Melchizedek

ELLEN GUNDERSON TRAYLOR

HARVEST HOUSE PUBLISHERS
Eugene, Oregon 97402

Scripture references are taken from the King James Version of the Bible.

Cover by Terry Dugan Design, Minneapolis, Minnesota.

MELCHIZEDEK

Copyright © 1997 by Harvest House Publishers
Eugene, Oregon 97402

Library of Congress Cataloging-in-Publication Data

Traylor, Ellen Gunderson.
  Melchizedek / Ellen Traylor.
     p.   cm.
  ISBN 1-56507-528-5
  1. Melchizedek, King of Salem—Fiction. 2. Bible. O.T.—History of Biblical events—Fiction. I. Title.
PS3570.R357M45   1997
813'.54—dc20

96-34330
CIP

Printed in the United States of America.

97 98 99 00 01 02 / BC / 10 9 8 7 6 5 4 3 2 1

There are those of Earth
whose beginning is humble
and whose way is hard,
but whose path leads to glory . . .
This story is for them.

To My Sons
Aaron and Nathan

*"A good name is rather to be chosen
than great riches."*
—Proverbs 22:1a

Contents

"Let this mind be in you, which was also in Christ Jesus: Who, being in the form of God, thought it not robbery to be equal with God: But made himself of no reputation, and took upon him the form of a servant."

—Philippians 2:5–7a

A Note to the Reader

Since the recent release of my archaeological novel, *Jerusalem—The City of God*, many people have asked me about Melchizedek, the city's founder. He is, of course, the first major character in that book and, because of the mystique surrounding him, readers are curious to know more.

This new book, *Melchizedek—King of Jerusalem*, fills in the narrative gap between my prehistorical novel, *Noah*, and *Jerusalem—the City of God*, detailing what Scripture, legend, lore, and rational deduction indicate to be the likely scenario of events following the Great Flood and Earth's repopulating.

Shortly after I finished writing *Noah*, findings in southeastern Turkey confounded traditional archaeology and threw into serious question premises that had for years been mainstays of scientific thought. Ten-thousand-year-old stone buildings, too advanced for "primitive" peoples to have constructed, were unearthed just miles from the mountain where the Ark touched down.

According to experts in Istanbul, and at the Oriental Institute of the University of Chicago, the findings suggest that folks living in the region had achieved a level of "social complexity" not previously encountered in explorations of early agricultural societies. Not only were the buildings a bewilderment, but industry, the arts, and mathematics were apparently more advanced than would be expected for the period.

To my delight, the findings support the theories that *Noah* propounded, giving evidence to a highly advanced society prior to the Great Flood. They also help lay a groundwork of understanding for the period that followed, in its religious practices as well as its technology.

If Noah's children had known the science and industry of the pre-Flood world (known variously as Adamlanda, Adlandia, and Atlantis, meaning "Land of Adam"), they would not long be satisfied with caves, with hunting and gathering. Nor would they be content without art and social structure.

It is interesting to note that scholars cannot pinpoint the "ethnic origins" of the Ararat findings. But if we believe that the people who descended from the Ark were the parents of the world as we know it, they were the "originals" themselves!

From them, society across the globe, in all its diversity, color, and history, derived.

It is the purpose of this volume to investigate those roots, to go back to the times of Shem, Ham, and Japheth, and to see what became of them. It is also my goal to give a plausible biography of Melchizedek, who left Ararat to found the Holy City.

Not only does the human family owe itself to the children of Noah, but our most fundamental understandings of God, of good and evil, have their beginnings in the experience of post-Flood clans.

In this work, as in its predecessor, I contend that the keys to many of the mysteries of Genesis and other parts of Scripture lie in the obscure period of the pre-Flood world and in the era of the new-born Earth that followed on its heels.

Three themes stand out in the very sketchy renderings of Genesis: the origin of the races, humankind's repeated choice between good and evil, and the ongoing contention between spiritual forces over the destiny of humanity.

These are awesome topics for any writer to tackle.

Therefore, this product, like *Noah* and *Jerusalem—The City of God*, is the result of intensive study. Building on the vast amount of research involved in *Noah*, I have continued to ferret out meaningful resources on the subsequent era.

I am grateful to my friend and noted "Ark-ologist," Dr. Charles D. Willis, of Fresno, California, for his insights into the Turkish language, and into the meaning of place names near Ararat, which illumine the story of Noah's children.

Because Scriptural information regarding this era is very sketchy, I draw support for some of my ideas from the lore and tradition of the Old Testament Pseudepigrapha, especially concerning the mysterious figure of Melchizedek.

I also drew inspiration from Don Richardson's comments regarding this enigmatic person, as put forth in his fine book, *Eternity in Their Hearts*. While my theories concerning Melchizedek may surprise many readers, I contend that the mystery surrounding him arises from his position of crucial prominence in the preservation of God-consciousness throughout the dark ages of our beginnings.

May the Lord honor my stumbling attempts to unravel things too deep for my finite imagination. And may He use His handmaid to bring honor to Himself.

To Jesus, The Author and Finisher of our Faith,

Ellen Traylor
Polson, Montana

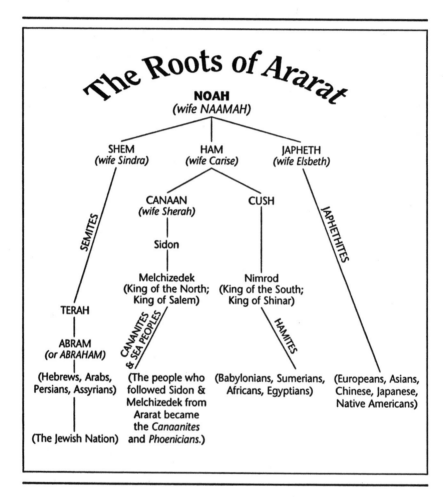

The Roots of Ararat

NOAH
(wife NAAMAH)

SHEM
(wife Sindra)

HAM
(wife Carise)

JAPHETH
(wife Elsbeth)

CANAAN
(wife Sherah)

CUSH

Sidon

Melchizedek
(King of the North;
King of Salem)

Nimrod
(King of the South;
King of Shinar)

TERAH

ABRAM
(or ABRAHAM)

(Hebrews, Arabs,
Persians, Assyrians)

(The people who
followed Sidon &
Melchizedek from
Ararat became
the *Canaanites*
and *Phoenicians*.)

(Babylonians, Sumerians,
Africans, Egyptians)

(Europeans, Asians,
Chinese, Japanese,
Native Americans)

(The Jewish Nation)

SEMITES

CANAANITES & SEA PEOPLES

HAMITES

JAPHETHITES

Prologue

A casual breeze ruffled the gauze curtains of King Melchizedek's chamber window, bringing the aroma of sage and myrtlewood up from the canyon floor. Even at this elevation, where the palace sat astride one steep cliff, the sound of the gently rushing Gihon Spring, the fount that had lured the first settlers to the area, could be heard.

It was nearing sunset, and time for the old monarch's evening repast. A small, dark-haired servant boy tiptoed quietly into the room, bowing as he entered, and carrying a tray of succulent fruit and cheese. He was too young to fully appreciate the honor of his position, but not too young to be in awe of the mysterious ruler.

Always, when he came into the master's presence, he did so quietly, sensing that the king would wish this. And more often than not, he found the old man seated at his window, peering up the long highway that ran through Canaan, as though he looked for someone.

This evening was no different. Placing the tray on a low olivewood table, the boy stood silently by, awaiting further instructions and secretly hoping the king might bid him sit a while.

Melchizedek had often done so, and those had been the most wonderful times of the lad's life, for the venerable man was a great teller of tales, a master weaver of legend and lore. And it seemed he had few confidants to grace with his stories.

Ali would not be surprised, however, if the king were to wave him off tonight. He knew that tomorrow was a most important day on the monarch's calendar, and that this evening he would likely prefer to sit alone.

Tomorrow was the annual Day of Atonement, when the mysterious king would perform a strange ritual upon the great table-rock that rose north of town, placing a platter of bread and wine before the modest temple erected there, and then offering up a small lamb to his deity. At the end of this act, he would always gaze across the fields of Canaan, surveying them from the height of the mount on which the

11

lamb had been slain. In his eyes would be eager hope, again as though he searched for someone. But he never said just who it was he sought, and when he turned to go back to the vale, taking his bread-laden tray with him, it was always with a look of disappointment.

What the ritual sprang from, and why the king insisted on it, was a question young Ali had never heard answered. The ceremony seemed not to be connected with any local god, but Melchizedek was highly revered, and the citizens of his small city-state observed his holiday out of deference to his position.

Regarding Melchizedek, there were *many* unanswered questions. No one really knew how long he had reigned over this parcel of earth. Some said that generations had come and gone since he first settled here. This alone provoked local folk and foreigners alike to marvel. But equally amazing was the fact that his town of Salem had never seen war.

Pocketed along a narrow canyon, and known simply as "The Valley of the King," or "The King's Dale," it had always been uncontested territory, belonging since time immemorial to this venerable old fellow.

Recently the land of Canaan, which surrounded his peaceful valley, had been greatly troubled by a Babylonian alliance, eastern kings who threatened to overrun the entire region. They had, in fact, managed to take numerous cities up and down the Jordan, from Damascus to the Salt Sea, and had then turned their weapons along the western bank.

Melchizedek, who had outlived many conquerors, regarded the matter with little concern. Even when he had been told that a young merchant prince from Mesopotamia had chased the culprits north, overwhelming them with a handful of crudely trained militia, he had shrugged it off as a military oddity.

Always, it seemed, he preferred to think of things deeper than politics and nations. Ali, who had been privileged to talk with the old man, knew that his interests inclined more to the past than to the present.

The servant boy was turning for the door, bowing out of the king's chamber, when suddenly the master, acknowledging his presence, whispered, "Do you hear the spring?"

Ali, surprised at the question, stood still and listened. The old king sat with his head cocked toward the open window, and at last the boy replied, "Yes, Majesty. It is like soft singing."

"But the sound of rushing water can sometimes be terrifying," the king suggested.

"Yes, if there is a great deal of it," the lad agreed.

"So it must have been during the Deluge."

The young servant had heard many stories of the universal flood, the one that had nearly destroyed the earth millennia before. He had heard them from his parents and from the myths of his nation. But the most fabulous tales regarding this ancient cataclysm he had heard from Melchizedek.

Though the king's stories involved demigods, strange creatures, and mighty works such as the world had not since seen, they rang truer to Ali than the preposterous legends of his people. Over and over he had requested Melchizedek to recount the tales of the Overlords, the superhuman beings who had once stalked the earth. He listened, rapt, as the king related accounts, handed down from his own ancestors, of sprawling cities, and harnessed energies that allowed men to fly and the sea to be mastered. He marveled at the twisted ends to which the powers had been put, and shuddered to think of the monstrosities that the demigods had created from the stuff of life.

Again and again he had drunk in the fables, which he knew were more than fables, and he had never tired of it.

But today, the king would speak of later things.

Lifting a piece of pomegranate from off his tea tray, Melchizedek grew more contemplative. Round and round he turned the juicy morsel in his wizened fingers, gazing upon it, but not really seeing it. And as he turned his pale face toward the sunset, he stroked his long white beard and sighed.

"Imagine . . . just imagine," he wondered, "what the earth must have been like as the waters receded. Imagine how the folk disembarking from the Ark must have trembled to see the ground, stripped of green, frothing with ooze."

"There were only a handful, sir, were there not?" the boy recalled.

"Yes," Melchizedek affirmed. "And they were lonely, Ali. The human race was lonely for itself."

The lad said nothing, his mind's eye envisioning the huddled family of Noah as they stood stark against the bleak mount upon which the great ship had come to rest.

Melchizedek rose from his cedar chair and set the untasted fruit upon the platter. Wiping his moist fingers absently upon his robe, he walked to the window and gazed out again. Ali could tell by his intent face that he was about to launch into a new installment of his history.

"Yes," he intoned, his voice gaining volume as he spoke, "if eight men and women and one little child could be called a 'race,' and if the void, muddy world, whose mountains had been turned to valleys and whose valleys had been reared skyward could be called the 'Earth'"—by now his arms were flung wide, and he seemed to speak to the hills beyond—"the remnant of humanity must refill it!"

Likely so, thought Ali, as he imagined those poor people longing to see their own existence reflected in the faces of others, longing for echoes of sympathetic speech.

Melchizedek glanced away from the arch and studied his little friend. "But, what were nine souls among the uncounted miles of this convoluted planet?" he demanded. "What impression could a handful of lonely creatures make upon an uncharted wilderness, whereon neither man nor beast had ever before set foot?"

His patriarchal beard shook as he asked this, his pale olive eyes lighting with zeal. Did he mean for Ali to answer him? The boy only sat mute.

"Impress it they must!" he asserted. Then, drawing close, he bent over the boy, his fingers fluttering like tongues of fire before his eyes. "They were born to it," he whispered, "as the spark flies upward from a flame, as the snows of Ararat fall down from the splotchy clouds that once formed Earth's canopy!"

The lad was breathless with the old man's poetry, mesmerized by the commanding description.

Matter-of-factly, Melchizedek pulled back and paced the room. "They were more inclined to fill and subdue than were their first parents," he explained, "when the planet was created for mankind. Adam and Eve were not born into population, industry, teeming cities, or progress."

No, thought the lad, *of course not.*

"Noah and his kin had always known such things," Melchizedek went on, punctuating the idea with a pointed finger. "And they bore in their veins the propensity to know them again!"

"*Did* they know them again, Master?" Ali asked. "Did Noah build a city?"

At this Melchizedek smiled, a wistful, pleasant smile.

"Ah, lad, the world was beautiful as the hills became green again, and the mountain quickly filled with people. It was not many years before the cities came. Sometimes they brought good and sometimes evil. But it was a God-given yearning that spurred folk to think grandly. It was the creative urge, borne of their kindredness with the Almighty."

What religion Melchizedek claimed seemed beyond definition. Numberless gods and goddesses were popular in Canaan. But when the king spoke of his deity, it was in the most elevated terms. His God he called "The Most High, Possessor of Heaven and Earth," and his own view of things seemed far grander than anyone else's.

Ali leaned forward, inquiringly. Never before had he asked a personal question of the king. Never had he interrupted one of his stories. But today he sensed what he had always sensed: that Melchizedek spoke firsthand, as though he had been very close to the history he recounted, and not born hundreds of years afterward.

"Sir," the lad dared, "tell me . . . how do you know these things? No one speaks as you do . . . no one . . ." .

Melchizedek smiled fondly at the youngster who had spent countless hours at his feet.

The azure light of nearing sunset gleamed about the old sage, shining upon his long white hair like a halo. The lad was speechless, but somehow found courage to address him once more.

"Sir, they say you have no beginning, that you have been here in the land of Canaan forever. They say you never had a father, and that you will live forever!"

Now Melchizedek's broad smile stretched his lips. "They say that, do they? People say such things for lack of knowledge. It is easy to say something does not exist simply because you have no record of it."

The boy was perplexed, as Melchizedek could see.

"Where, lad, do you suppose the name of this land came from? Has anyone ever told you about Canaan?"

"Why, yes, sir," the boy recalled. "*You* told me. That was the name of the baby—the one Noah cursed!"

"Yes, my child," the king laughed, tears glimmering along his grey lashes. "But if I speak of Canaan, I must begin again with Noah."

At this, Melchizedek went to his cedar chair and took his seat. Leaning back, he closed his eyes.

"And if I speak of Canaan, I will surely speak also of myself . . ."

PART I

"And the sons of Noah, that went forth of the ark, were Shem, and Ham, and Japheth: and Ham is the father of Canaan."

—Genesis 9:18

A Servant of Servants

—1—

p from the twilight plain, a moist wind blew, bringing the lingering scent of mud and decay. Noah had never become accustomed to the smell, not in the three years since the Ark had landed, and he had first set foot in the new world.

As dusk deepened toward night, he sat alone on the ridge at the Ark's foot, gazing sadly across the bleak wilderness.

His black and comely wife, Naamah, glanced furtively through the curtain of her hut door, disappointed to see that Noah had not changed positions since last she checked on him.

She knew what thoughts possessed him. She knew the ache of his broken heart, for it was hers as well.

The heavy sting of words spoken this day upon the mountain still rang in her ears. As she peered down the hill of the new world's first village, which future generations would call Heshton, meaning "village of the eight survivors," she glimpsed the small stone houses of the other family members. She knew Noah's harsh pronouncement against Ham, the middle son, echoed in their hearts likewise.

Her eldest and youngest sons, Shem and Japheth, and their wives had kept to themselves all evening, doubtless pondering the prophecy the bearded patriarch had hurled across the valley.

She understood the tortured emotions that had driven the preacher to make the proclamation. She also knew that he, being a man of God, was provoked to this conclusion by more than personal pride.

Across her mind's eye, Ham's persistent image stalked with defiant strides. Never would she forget the witness of his departure, as he had loaded all his belongings upon a small cart and lifted his wife, Carise, to the plank seat. The usually free-spirited girl had pleaded with fear-filled eyes for someone to intervene. But it was no use. Her husband was determined to leave and her fiery temper was tamed to

19

bewildered silence. Upon her lap she cradled the couple's squalling infant, little Canaan, target of the prophecy.

"Beware, Ham," Noah had warned, his voice trumpetlike, "lest your glory turn to dust. One day your unforgiving heart will be your ruin, and Canaan shall bear the curse. A servant of servants shall he be to his brothers!"

Thus had years of bitterness culminated, the rift that had grown slowly and deeply between Noah and Ham since his childhood brought into sharp focus.

A few months before, on the night of Canaan's birth, Ham had committed the ultimate crime against his father. Noah had stumbled from the campfire, tipsy from drinking prematurely fermented wine and dazed from celebrating the first birth in the new world. Disgracefully, he had stripped himself to the skin and had fallen asleep in his tent. Ham, finding him in this obscene state, had chosen to make a spectacle of him, calling to his brothers and bidding them, "Come, see the righteous prophet!"

But this had been only the climactic evidence of tension and resentment that had festered in Ham for years. And, Naamah knew, his resentments were not without foundation.

If she had hoped life in the new world might obliterate the evils of the past, she had been quickly disillusioned. Even within the Ark itself, as it rocked and heaved upon the waters of God's wrath, contentions had flowered. And when the first family, the only family to survive the Flood, had set about to plant their lives in the muddy dirt, they had sown seeds of strife plucked from the soil of the past.

Too aware of this now, Naamah turned from the window with a sigh. As she wistfully drew the curtain across the hut door, she sought in vain to shut out thoughts of her favorite son, of the dusky Ham, who had been closest to her of all her children.

—2—

The small wooden-wheeled cart rumbled down the southern slope of Ararat, hobbling over the debris of rocks and stubby plants raised obstinately above the silty flood layer.

Ham led the cart's strong-muscled ox by a short muzzle strap. The animal's large, shining eyes carefully surveyed the trailless ground beneath its hooves as it picked its way across the plain, much too slowly for its impatient master.

The little babe, Canaan, resting in his mother's arms, competed against the jolting crunch of wheel upon stone with lusty cries. Carise quickly bared her milk-laden breast and the infant turned instinctively for the soft warm flesh, nuzzling to contented silence.

The woman studied her husband's heedless back, where it glistened beneath the unveiled sun in a sweat that accentuated his dark skin. A sigh of conflicting emotions filled her, love and hate competing for her heart.

Neither the man nor the woman knew their destination. Oh, Ham had spoken of some glorious land to the south and east, upon which he had come in his hunting trips—a land he called Shinar. But what life could mean for them there, neither really knew. Though she might have asked him, she dared not. And he volunteered nothing.

Carise would never forget how her husband had raised his fist to his father's face—how just this morning he had spurned Noah's God and taken off from the small family group on the mountain.

The resultant prophecy, hurled from Noah's constricted throat, still thundered in her soul: "Cursed be Canaan! A servant of servants shall he be!"

As she pondered these words, she stiffened, and the babe nursing at her bosom jerked away, his face screwed in an indignant scowl, his angry cry again breaking the silence.

Of Noah's three sons, Ham had been the rebel. By a mere cast of the genetic die, he, of the three brothers, bore the closest physical kinship to his mother's racial strain. Though Noah had broken tradition, ripping away years of taboo by falling in love with and marrying a Cainite woman, old legacies of prejudice and doubt had persistently driven themselves between the prophet and Ham, until the lad eschewed all attempts to find a secure place in his father's estimation.

Even now, as he led his tiny family forth, Ham's stormy eyes radiated brooding anticipation. Anger was his soulmate, along with a fistful of shell-hard pride.

Though Canaan's cries stabbed at Carise's fear-wracked heart, they charged Ham with zeal. His son was a strong one—lusty and fine. He would raise him to pound against heaven—to call down glory on their heads and on the heads of all their descendants.

• • •

Quiet . . . sometimes Carise felt she would go mad from the quiet!

The new country to which her husband had brought her was a vacuum of solitude. He had named it Shinar, meaning "shining land," but she called it Silence.

Now and then, Carise wondered if her past life was only an unlived dream; if she were, in truth, the only woman on earth, sprung full-grown from the silty soil outside her cave.

Today, she knelt beside the fire pit in the black depths of the cave that had been home since Ham brought her from Ararat.

Though it had been only three years, it seemed a lifetime had elapsed since she had followed her husband down the mountain's southern valley. Between two immense rivers they had wended, through a land as lush as Ham had reported it to be.

Except for the small child, Canaan, who was bedded down upon a pallet of animal pelts, the woman was alone. Such was her condition all too often, as Ham trekked far from camp evening after evening, in quest of game.

One thing, only, assured her that she had not always been an exile, that her memories were real. That one thing was the child, the sole evidence that she had once had a family. Canaan had Grandmother Naamah's deep, pleasant eyes and Grandfather Noah's intelligence. Though he was almost as dark-skinned as Ham, aspects of his uncles sparked in his playfulness and in his lithe, strong body.

The toddler had just been weaned. On Ararat, such an event would have been cause for great celebration. Naamah and the three sisters-in-law would have worked for days, baking and cooking, preparing a feast for the family. Noah would have practiced a dynamic speech with which to usher Canaan out of infancy and into childhood, a speech full of references to God who was the boy's protector and guide, and to the future that held all the promise of a world just beginning.

Ham and his brothers would have spent weeks fashioning gifts for the boy: a spear, a shield, a knife, weapons of survival in a land where game was not yet abundant and where the offspring of the very animals that had been the Ark's cargo now had a healthy fear of predatory humans.

The women would have woven a new blanket for Canaan, one to serve as both cloak and bedding as he left off sleeping with his mother and had his own pallet. Naamah would have made him new moccasins, which could stretch for several months as he grew.

It would have been a merry time, reminiscent of celebrations in the old world, among the Sethite race who were the remnant that still retained the worship of Yahweh.

Though Noah and his sons were the only ones, even among the Sethites, who were true believers, such celebrations involved whole villages and went on for days, culminating in the presentation of the youngster to God as an independent being, ready to be taught righteousness.

But the weaning of Canaan had been witnessed only by his mother. Not even Ham, away hunting, had been present when her decision to release the child had been made. That decision had been necessary because she was once again pregnant. It was a minor miracle that a nursing woman should conceive. But it had happened, and being alone when her condition became clear, she made the decision to wean without fanfare.

All of this had been hard for Carise, precipitating even more sense of isolation and loneliness.

Tonight, however, she was actually grateful for her solitude. Between the flashing flames of the cave fire, melancholy memories danced, recollections of herself as a girl, in swirling robes and golden bangles, weaving and swaying through the orange glow of her father's caravan fire.

Against the cave wall leaned a makeshift loom upon which she had attempted repeatedly to weave fabrics reminiscent of the colorful garb to which she was accustomed. Though she had improved upon the simple material that sheep's wool provided, she had never quite matched the tints of Adlandian dyes, and the designs she managed to create seemed dull by comparison.

In fact, everything about this new world was wretched, she had concluded.

Even now, up the valley, she could hear the all-too-familiar rumbling of the Earth as it moved nervously underfoot. This, or an occasional animal cry, were the only noises that broke days of silence. Crawling toward her son, she huddled above him protectively, and braced herself, as she had learned to do, in anticipation of a tremor.

How many times she had experienced such seismic phenomena she could never count. But she had not become used to them. The very mountains were unstable, unlike the sturdy ranges of the pre-Flood world. As she gripped the floor against a sudden lurch of the ground, she called Ham's name through gritted teeth.

The fearsome changes in the terrain and in the climate had not been so terrifying when she dwelt on Ararat. There she had shared each startling newness with her loved ones, Noah's family. But here she too often had no one.

The planet's virgin soil had yielded up tender plants and already the hills sported infant forests and eager jungles. But with the greening, devastating upheavals visited the landscape, spikes of granite forcing themselves up through canyon floors, or great ridges crashing to valley bottoms at the slightest shudder.

Carise, who remembered a world of perfectly temperate climes, had confronted sleet and hail and beating sun. She had seen land bloom as a rose one month only to be replaced by arid crust the next.

Just now, she prayed to the God of Noah, petitioning for safety and hoping that the cave home would not collapse with the next swell.

At last calm descended, and cautiously she pulled back from Canaan's sleeping form.

The solitude was again loathsome. Wiping her tear-smudged face, Carise returned to the fire and knelt before the warm embers.

Long black shadows cast her image against the walls, and she saw the gentle swell of her own abdomen. By early spring she would bear Ham this second child, but the thought only compounded her sense of despair.

She knew that a woman's doldrums were upon her, the mental state above which it was hard to rise in early pregnancy. Ham would have reminded her of this, had he been available. But memories of the old world and of her happiness there tormented her.

Turning to the loom against the wall, she contemplated once more just how she might create some color for herself. Valley berries and flowers were becoming more abundant each spring. Perhaps next year she would harvest the saffron and cobalt dyes she craved, or the tinge of scarlet that raged through her reveries.

But by then, she realized, she would again be a nursing mother, and she would be weary—too weary to go collecting.

Until recently she had nurtured the belief that captivity in this alien land would soon be ending. Despite Ham's insistence that his destiny lay here, she had never taken the notion seriously. Surely, she had assumed, he would tire of this exile, and return to his people.

Tonight, as she sat with her sleeping child and felt the stirring of life within her womb, apprehension overwhelmed hope.

Canaan was old enough to need playmates. Soon he would begin to ask questions, and she wondered how she would answer them.

"Yes," she would tell him, "there are other people on Earth . . . No, we never see them . . . Yes, I know you are lonely . . . I know. . . ." But how to explain such a situation to a little boy, she could not imagine.

Then, too, he would not always be little. One day, he would ask bigger questions, and he would begin to make demands.

Fear projected her into the future, to a time when the lad would have need of things that neither she nor Ham could provide—an extended family, the companionship of peers, and human love beyond the love of parents.

Sadly she crawled again to the boy, whose breathing came slow and even, and whose dreamy countenance defied such worries.

With a gentle hand she stroked his cool brow and brushed his cheek with a kiss.

Despite his quiet repose, Carise could think only of the curse. And as she surveyed the beloved features of her firstborn, her heart ached for him, with a heaviness only a mother could know.

—3—

A

t fourteen, Canaan was a strong, comely lad who enjoyed a close relationship with his father. His parents and his sister, born when he was four, had been his only companions as he grew to manhood.

This afternoon he squatted beside his father upon a ridge overlooking the Hiddekel (or "rapid") River, one day to be called Tigris. Together they scanned the plain below with keen eyes, watching a herd of gazelles grazing along the banks of the wide, silver ribbon.

A gentle wind played against their backs, coming from the direction of Ararat, whose peak was lost in the vast distance separating them from all other humans. As the breeze passed over their shoulders, carrying their scent to the wary creatures below, the lead buck lifted his head and sniffed the air.

It was this very movement the hunters had awaited. Quickly, Canaan poised his bow and let fly a perfectly aimed arrow. No sooner had it left the string than the buck slumped to its knees.

"There was no pain," Ham said with a nod, praising his son's marksmanship. "A proper kill allows its quarry a peaceful death."

Canaan's face lit in a broad smile. He relished nothing greater than his father's approval, which he had had in hefty doses all his life.

With deft strides the two descended the ridge, running upon the herd as it scattered wildly and sinking to the ground beside the gazelle's unbreathing body. No further word passed between them as they eagerly tied the fore and hind legs with sinew thongs and passed a long staff between the knots.

They would not stop to clean the carcass just now. The sun would soon be setting and they did not wish to stay another night in the field. With easy strength they hoisted the prey between them, Canaan at the rear and Ham at the front. Bearing the staff upon their shoulders, they began the slow trek back up the ridge.

When they reached the top, Ham stopped to rest a moment and as he did so he observed Canaan's wistful glance toward the hazy realms northwest, toward the sunset mountain from which all life had disembarked. And he felt he knew the contents of his son's heart.

A spur of jealousy nudged him, With practiced skill he turned the lad's thoughts toward his own dreams.

"See how the water catches the departing sun?" the hunter directed. "All this valley catches the sun and holds it in its bosom through each night." Ham bent over to scoop up a heap of soil between his fingers. Holding it forth, he bid Canaan take it.

"What do you feel, my boy?" he urged.

Canaan's face was quizzical. "I feel dirt," was his simple reply.

Ham's brow knit in disappointment. "But, more than that!" he insisted. "Is the soil not warm?"

"Yes," Canaan assented. "It is warm."

"You hold within your hand rays of the sun itself, where the soil has captured it!" Then turning the youngster's attention again to the valley floor, Ham explained, "This is the most fertile land on Earth! Kissed daily by the light of heaven. This, my boy, is *our* land, whereon we shall raise up mighty empires!"

The lad had heard it all before, countless times. Canaan tried to echo his father's enthusiasm as he said, "Indeed, we shall."

He knew the definition of an empire by the tales Ham had told regarding lost Adlandia. And he knew the meaning of "mighty" by the stories of the Overlords, which his father often rehearsed.

As the men lifted the carcass once again upon their shoulders and headed home, Canaan dared to ask a deep thing. "Did you worship the sun, Father, before the Great Rains came?"

Ham winced, but looked straight ahead as he walked. "Why do you ask this?" he inquired.

"Mother says. . ."

"Mother should say less than she does!" Ham interrupted. "What else does Mother say?"

There was a bitter edge to the question. But Canaan tried not to grow defensive. "She says," he went on, "that not all men worshipped the sun. She says that my grandfather and your brothers worshipped another . . ."

Ham turned an angry face toward Canaan, and the lad left the sentence incomplete.

Ahead, in the dim twilight, they discerned the orange glow that marked the mouth of their family cave. As they drew nearer, they could see the silhouettes of Carise and her daughter as they tended the fire and made preparations for the hoped-for meal.

Ham lifted his nose to the wind, just as the gazelle had done, and his lips curled in satisfaction. Already a savory broth of herbs and yams awaited the meat that would complete a ruddy stew.

The westland was lost to the darkness as Canaan followed his father into the rock-walled home. Quiet chatter filled the evening, the deer was cleaned, and a heavy red porridge simmered until their stomachs growled.

But the boy posed no more questions. Only in his imagination did he ponder the mysteries of the world and traipse the slopes of Ararat.

C arise stood in the cave door, resting from the heat of midday. Her son, and Keilah, his sister, worked the small garden plot from which the family had enjoyed bounteous harvests since settling here.

Always before, the woman had observed their willing work with pride. Today, however, something in their aspects troubled her.

She watched as thirteen-year-old Keilah knelt in the rich soil and pulled up yet another weed. It was a blistering day, and the girl's bronze skin shone sweaty in the sunlight. Pushing a tousle of lustrous black hair back from her damp neck, Keilah swatted at a persistent fly and peered overhead at the tormenting sun.

Just then a little dirt clod, teasingly tossed in her direction, sent a spray of dust against her bare thigh. Brushing the silty stain from her skin, she glanced angrily at Canaan, but he busied himself in "innocent" preoccupation with his weeding.

Moments later a handful of grass splatted against the girl's sweat-streaked back, and though she kept her eyes to the hoe, the boy grilled her with his gaze until her face burned.

Though quiet by nature, Keilah had never been one to shy away from the frolic of sibling play. Her mother, however, could see that Canaan's brotherly fondness was laced with nervous agitation, and his typically attentive attitude was unusually strained.

Witnessing her children's peculiar interchange, Carise tried to convince herself that her fears were unfounded. But her heart was pricked, as it had been frequently of late, by their unnatural predicament.

The familiar anger she had stifled for years toward her husband, Ham, brought the blood to her cheeks. And her own face burned.

Suddenly, a quick movement on Keilah's part demanded attention. The girl had thrown down her hoe and headed for the water pot in the shade of the cave hill. When she came near, Carise detected tears along her lashes.

The woman wisely waited a moment before approaching her daughter. Should she be imagining the child was distressed, she did not wish to suggest to her a problem. But now she could hear the girl's quiet sobs, and knew she must intervene.

"Keilah, what happened in the field?" she inquired.

The girl glanced up, her moist eyes soft like those of a young doe. She pondered the question before answering it, and at last, with a sigh, replied, "Nothing."

Carise absorbed the guileless response. "Canaan has been unkind!" she insisted. Turning for the field, she proclaimed, "I will speak with him!"

But Keilah grasped her by the arm. "No, mother," she pleaded. "It is nothing. My brother is never unkind."

Carise, frustrated, sighed. "But, you are crying. If he neither said nor did anything to upset you, why are you troubled?"

Keilah looked away toward her brother for a brief moment. The strong lad, his torso gleaming in the hot sun, had not lifted his focus from the plow. But the girl trembled as though he watched her even now.

Replying not a word, she suddenly pulled back and headed for a grove of shady trees, not far distant, leaving Carise to contemplate the situation.

Despairing, the mother retreated through the cave door, but cast a final glance toward Canaan.

As she suspected, he was peering covertly up from his work, watching Keilah's departure, and caught helplessly by his sister's feminine gait.

• • •

When Ham came home that night from the day's hunt, he found Carise in a singular mood. In fact the atmosphere of the entire evening was heavy with brooding silence.

Canaan picked at his meal, despite the fact that he should have worked up a fierce appetite, sweating all afternoon in the field.

Keilah sat in the shadows, barely uttering a sound until she crept off to bed ahead of the others.

When the youngsters had fallen asleep, Carise lay awake, tossing upon the great bear skin that she and Ham shared near the cave mouth. When her husband reached for her, she coldly pulled away.

"It is not a good thing . . ." she murmured.

Ham listened with care, hoping to hear the cause of his wife's rebuff. But when Carise said nothing more, he sighed and reached for her rigid body once again. "What, Carise . . ." he whispered, "what is not a good thing?"

With an angry jerk, she turned toward him, glaring through the narrow space of dark that separated them. "You are not blind!" she growled. "Can't you see what is happening beneath your very nose?"

"Perhaps not," he smiled. Raising her obstinate fingers to his lips, he caressed them fondly. "You have always been more observant than I. What is it?"

Carise heaved a sigh. "You are a man. Surely you recognize the stirrings within your own son! We must find him a wife, before something disgraceful happens!"

Ham grew silent. Carise listened a long time for a response. When it came, she was appalled.

A chuckle began as a low rumble, issuing from her husband's throat, growing in volume until he was sitting up on the bed, holding his sides with hilarity.

"Keilah?" he managed between bouts of laughter. "You speak of Keilah and Canaan?"

"I do!" the woman barked. "Have you noticed the tension between them?"

Ham rose from the pallet and walked to the cave door, yawning and stretching in the moonlight. When he left the rocky room, wandering toward the garden, Carise followed him.

"What did you think would be the outcome of our isolation?" the woman demanded. "Did you think we could raise two lonely children, a boy and a girl, without . . ."

"Woman!" Ham bellowed, turning on her. "Nothing has happened yet!"

"You are right. Not 'yet'!" she returned, her black eyes catching moonfire.

Ham grew sullen and spoke no more for a long while. At last, when he did give his opinion, Carise was unprepared for the intimation.

"So . . ." he whispered, looking up and away to the dark heavens, "what if our son and daughter did take pleasure? Such a thing has been known to happen . . ."

The woman stared at him in numb horror. "You would speak blessing on such an act?" She trembled.

"This is a new world, the world beginning again," Ham asserted. "You have heard that when our first parents bore sons and daughters, brother married sister! Why, the wife of Seth was his own sister, Azura, was she not? And Noam bore Enos fine sons! Even our forefather, Cain, took Awan with him to Nod!"

Carise shook her head, and drew back, feeling more alien from him than ever before. "Hypocrisy!" she shouted. "You speak the truth regarding our first parents. But those were different times than these, and the choices far fewer! Yahweh does not bless such unions now!"

Ham turned his back to the rebuke, but then she was at his side, grasping him by the arm, wheeling him about. "You would accept any folly if it precluded your returning to your father!" she cried. "More than likely daughters have been born to Shem and Japheth. Yet, you would allow your own children to stumble, rather than swallow your pride!"

The man stared across the garden and past the plain bordering the great river. Tears nudged at his lashes, but he hid them stubbornly. "I have dreams," he insisted. "A dusky race to fill my kingdom . . ."

"Spawned by incest?" Carise spat. "Such a legacy for your descendants!"

Ham cast his gaze to the ground, and his shoulders slumped a little. "I never thought deeply on it . . ." he confessed.

As the woman studied him, considering his self-imposed quandary, an ache replaced the anger in her heart. She reached forth a hand to touch him, but then, drawing back, raised her chin in firm resolve.

"It is time, my lord, to think deeply on many things. Dreams are precious, but not if they are built on illusion."

Ham lifted his eyes to hers. "Ararat?" he whispered.

"Before the next full moon," the woman replied. "You must leave for Ararat within the month!"

—5—

The ox moved even more slowly when Ham returned to the Ark's mountain than when he had left. Not only was the up-hill grade a hindrance, but the cart was loaded more heavily this time.

During the month allotted before Ham left on the quest, Keilah and Carise had created numerous gifts for the unknown bride: fabrics in riotous colors and weaves, pottery of riverbank clay, jewelry of carved bone and hammered leather. Yesterday they had laden the cart with the riches, and Canaan and Ham had added to the bounty hand-made spears and bows, dried meat, fleeces from their flocks and shining smooth deerskins. Honed-flint arrowheads glistened atop the weapons and on the tips of arrowshafts.

All of this was bride-price, payment to the patriarch and the girl's father in exchange for her hand in marriage.

Small shields, constructed of wooden frames overstretched with rigid leather, topped the cargo. The shields were not for war, for there was no war upon Earth, but they were symbolic of manhood. Ham had made three at Carise's suggestion—one for Noah, one for Shem, and one for Japheth. But he had done so with resentment. There was no part of him that wished to honor his brothers with such gifts.

Canaan would have accompanied Ham on the journey. In fact, he had greatly desired to go along. But his mother and sister could not be left alone that long in the wilderness.

Ham would never forget his last glimpse of the boy, who watched from the rise above the cave until his father was lost to sight. He felt he knew the lad as no man had ever known a son, and yet sometimes he wondered, when he observed his wistfulness, just what dreams possessed him.

Carise often complained that Ham understood Canaan no more than Noah had understood Ham. She accused Ham of projecting his own ambitions upon an unwilling heart.

But, he reasoned even now, the woman spoke foolishness. How could the boy, beautiful as the forests of Adlandia, not think as one of his blood must think?

Emotion forever overruled logic in Ham's heart. Despite the fact that Shem, Japheth and Ham had the same parents, Ham was proud to be the "dark son" and proud that Canaan was the dark son's son. He had convinced himself that he and Canaan were destined to reach the skies.

Still, it was a shame that Canaan must unite with a daughter of Ararat to begin the Kingdom of Shinar. Ham kicked at a pebble in his path as he tugged on the ox's strap. Pottery vessels slammed against swollen wineskins and clanked hollow upon the wagon's sides, reminding him of his purpose.

His fists clenched. Though part of him had always known this trip would one day be required, he resented it as he resented his father. And every step was a labor.

• • •

It was a full month's journey from Shinar to Ararat, even under the most favorable conditions. Ham had made the trip once before, after spying out the land of his dreams years earlier, and then he had taken his wife and newborn son back along the same path to establish a home in the Tigris Valley. But with the slowgoing this time, he could not be certain just when he would come upon Noah's camp.

Four days ago he had caught his first glimpse of the Ark's mighty mountain. And three days later he had begun to ascend its foothills.

The sun, blasting over Ararat's eastern rim, jolted him awake after his sixtieth night on the trail, and shielding his eyes against it, he surveyed his whereabouts.

Suddenly, his heart stopped in midbeat as the square nose of a gigantic barge, jutting out from a high crevice, caught his eye.

The Ark! Memories of a hundred sorts flooded through him. Recollections of the countless days spent cloistered within the vessel's bowels, in fellowship with his father and brothers, nudged his hardened heart. Peaceful days those had been, the most peaceful of their times together. But how quickly they had vanished, once the craft scraped ground!

It had been necessary that distance be established, he had told himself—distance between Noah's soul and his own. There had been great things to pursue. And family love would only intrude.

Standing up, he shook the nostalgia from his mind, spread his woolly mantle over his shoulders and grasped his staff in a firm hand. "Come!" he muttered to the ox.

The wagon jerked to a slow roll behind him, and he began his last few steps up the slope. He tried to imagine how he would explain his long absence to his kin.

But perhaps, after all these years, they cared not to hear an explanation.

—6—

Noah braced a chisel against a flat piece of stone wedged between his feet and lifted another rock to strike the tool's handle. With a firm blow he chipped a large fragment from the stone's smooth surface, and then moved the chisel's tip to the adjacent lip. Repeatedly he performed this task, positioning the tool, striking it and removing a sliver of compounded crust, until he had a sharp-honed edge along the implement.

Already he had broken off two larger hunks to provide a grasping place. All that remained was to refine the edge and smooth out the grip.

Placing the stone beside him, he eyed it scrupulously. This piece would serve as a hand-adze for scraping hides, or for crude chopping and cutting activities. He had developed variations on its style for ax and hatchet heads, spear and arrowheads, and so forth. After many experiments, he had learned over the years the best type of stone for each tool. But oh, how artless were such designs!

His father, Lamech, while never condoning the advanced technology of his time, would have pitied Noah such crude artifacts. The finest of metals had composed the machinery of the Lamechtown mill, and only the most coveted woodworking and carpentry tools had graced his shops.

Noah was grateful that his wife's brother was not here to see his pathetic collection. Tubal-Cain, arch-artisan of Adlandian metalworkers, would have blushed to see the toolmaking industry sink so low.

But Noah was not trained in metallurgy, nor was he a skilled cutler. As the knives, chisels, hammers, and planes brought aboard the Ark had succumbed to rust and overuse, the men of his family sought to replace them. But Shem and Japheth were no more gifted in such arts than their father, so gradually, stones and sticks were employed.

Noah glanced up the rise to the Ark, which brooded over the valley like a sleepy sentinel. The lacquer that had once sheened its sides, had dulled over the years. But apart from this sign of wear, it still stood sturdy and straight as the day it was borne aloft by the ascending floodwaters.

"A fine vessel she was!" Noah consoled himself. "I *am* a craftsman . . . of sorts. . . ."

Every timber composing the Ark was hand-hewn. If he only had the means, the mountain lumber and the instruments of design, he could craft a *city* to his wishes!

Indeed, at the rate his family was growing, a city would be necessary in a few years. Perhaps several cities. Sindra had already borne Shem three daughters and four sons, and Elsbeth had given Japheth two sets of twins, a boy and girl each, as well as a son and daughter. Some of these were ready to think of families of their own. Soon, dozens of grandchildren and great grandchildren would be spreading down the mountain.

Down the mountain . . .

Noah's thoughts suddenly turned to Ham, and to the heartbreak of his departure so long before. The aging father, ever since, had felt a hollow place in his soul.

Rising from the little pile of broken granite, Noah laughed sadly to himself. His heart, since Ham's going, was not unlike that splintered rock. The remaining core was still useful, but rough around the edges, hammered and chiseled by wounding blows. It would be as impossible to reconstruct it as to bring the fragments of this battered stone together again.

"We must make do with what we have," he shrugged.

As he turned to enter his abode, where he would rest from the morning heat, something down the plain caught his eye. Raising his arm against the blinding sun, he stopped short, incredulous.

Across the slope there ascended a dark stranger, followed closely by a wagon. The patriarch strained his vision, but . . . surely some devil deceived him. . . .

As the figure grew closer, however, and as he paused in the way, staring with equal awe at the hoary-headed one who watched from the door, Noah knew his identity.

"Ham . . ." he whispered.

Like firebrands, his legs were shot with energy. With agility he had not known in years, he ran from the house, across the hill and toward the wagon.

When he had nearly reached it, he stopped still, afraid to step closer. Tears brimmed in his eyes.

Only when Ham bowed upon one knee, fearing to meet his gaze, did the patriarch speak.

"Perhaps even old hearts can be mended . . ." he said, likewise kneeling and taking Ham in his arms.

Noah's middle son was silent as the elder embraced him, his heart a jumble. As his father wept aloud upon his neck, he returned the embrace and resisted his own tears.

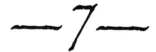

E ighteen years of separation may have mellowed Noah's feelings toward Ham, but Shem and Japheth were anything but warm toward the prodigal. Bitterly aloof, they sat in the clan's longhouse, glaring at the newcomer across the evening fire, offering no conversation and asking nothing about life in Shinar.

A curl of pungent smoke rose through the draft hole high overhead, and the golden blaze sent light to each corner of the council hall. As the Ararat clan had grown, this building, constructed years before by Noah and his sons, had been a necessity. Nineteen men, women, and children who enjoyed one another's company, and who spent more time together than apart, had required such a structure for feasts and councils.

While each family had its own stone cottage, Noah had decided that Yahweh would not be displeased if a few pieces of the Ark's siding were relegated to the meeting house.

It had been difficult for the patriarch to allow even this slight dismantling of the vessel. As guardian of the sacred ship, he suffered some guilt over his decision. But he and his sons vowed that this would be the only time they would use the priceless property for such a purpose. "Stone and rock," they had promised, "shall henceforth be our materials, until the Lord blesses us with new resources."

The old prophet was grateful for the pleasant structure which the gopherwood had provided—especially on evenings like this, when the building rang with sounds of life. Tonight, despite Shem's cold reserve and Japheth's pointed snubbing, the old man was most appreciative of the gathering place.

As Ham sat cross-legged, staring into the leaping flames, his face touched almost preternaturally by the orange glow, his father studied him privately. *How beautiful he is!* the old man considered.

Naamah had not been far from her son's side since his return, keeping close to him as a shadow, her black eyes full of pride and her voice like nectar whenever she called his name. Just now she bent over him, filling his half-empty cup and stroking his smooth brow with a tender hand. Noah's soul was full with the witness, as though, indeed, the past could be laid to rest.

But, he must steel his heart. Ham had been straightforward regarding his purpose here, and Noah must not delude himself that the lad intended to stay. Still, he reasoned, perhaps since the wandering one had set foot upon Ararat, his pride had softened.

Throughout the evening, Ham observed the activities of the women about the room. The elder daughters of Shem and Japheth, four in all, especially drew his notice. Any one of them could make a fine bride for Canaan. In fact, it would be difficult to choose among them.

His brothers knew nothing of Ham's purpose on the mount. Noah had not spoken of it, waiting for the evening meal to be completed before he broached the topic. It was not an easy subject to address, for it was a notion to which neither brother would take kindly.

When Japheth's daughter, Sherah, entered the fire-lit circle, her arms laden with driftwood collected from the floodplain, and when she bent down to feed the fire her father grew uneasy. He did not like the way Ham observed her.

As for the girl, she seemed oblivious to the drama being played out. She did not know that her crimson hair and mellow blue eyes could create a rivalry.

She was too fair-complected for Ham's taste, but she was indeed beautiful, and at least she was Japheth's daughter, not Shem's. Ham's animosity toward his eldest brother was unbounded.

"This one . . ." he simply said, turning to the patriarch.

Noah's eyes grew wide. "This one?" he stammered. "But she is the youngest of all. Her mother's heart would break!"

Ham was unyielding, as he had been countless times in his youth.

Suddenly, Japheth, interpreting the proceedings, drew up defiantly. "Elsbeth," he called, motioning for his wife, "Tell Sherah to fetch more wine! We are running low."

"But we just filled your cups," the buxom lady objected.

"Do as I say!" Japheth barked.

Elsbeth complied. "Come, Daughter," she called, giving her husband a perplexed scowl.

Sherah leaned away from the fire, aware now that her future was at stake. Casting a fearful glance at Ham, she departed.

Noah, seeing the set of Japheth's jaw, pulled close. "My sons," he spoke quickly, "your brother comes to Ararat with a petition. Canaan is now of marriageable age. He needs a wife. . ."

"Let him find one in Shinar!" Japheth spat. "No daughter of mine will marry a Hamite!"

"Nor mine!" Shem interjected. "The prodigal returns without repentance. Let him go out again, as he has come . . . with nothing!"

Japheth sat back, snorting, "I supposed that by now Ham had established his mighty kingdom! Did he perhaps forget the facts of life? Or did he expect to build his race on Carise's magic?"

Shem laughed hilariously, and Ham lurched forward, flinging epithets. "Don't you think I have always known I must one day return?" he growled. "I relish the necessity no more than you! Why, Canaan is too good for any of your pallid offspring!" he declared, clenching his fists. "But I am bound by the ways of God!"

"The ways of God?" Japheth hooted. "Since when do the ways of God concern you?"

"Enough!" Noah cried, raising his hands and parting the men who leaned over the fire. Then more softly, "It appears the old wounds have not healed."

"For *me*, never!" Shem assured him. "How can you welcome this renegade?"

Smitten, Naamah entered the council circle. "Hypocrites—all of you!" she railed. "You address the ways of God? As I understand it, God's way is forgiveness! Even the Flood spared a remnant of humankind. Yet you would wish death to Ham's seed, forever!"

Silence filled the chamber. Shem and Japheth stared, shamefaced, at the floor. Even Noah, realizing he had neglected to invoke God's blessing on the proceedings, was chagrined.

But at last, Shem objected. "Forgiveness *is* the Lord's way," he agreed. "But Ham has asked no forgiveness. Neither is he repentant!"

At this, everyone focused again on Ham, awaiting his rebuttal. When he said nothing, Naamah sighed.

Finally, Japheth placed a hand on his father's knee and challenged, "Would you have one of your granddaughters share the curse of Canaan?"

Noah's ears burned. How he longed for Yahweh's intervention!

But, as he considered the dilemma, he suddenly found himself speaking a strange thing—words that made no sense just now.

"A curse often contains the seed of blessing."

As the little audience deliberated upon this riddle, a hush again filled the chamber. Only the crackling fire intruded on the silence, until Noah, rising to his feet, grasped Ham by the arm and drew him up.

Staring him full in the face, with a posture of unquestioned authority, he commanded, "Sherah shall be bride to Canaan on one condition. You shall not take her from this mountain, but shall bring your family hence to live. And if you ever leave again, Canaan and his wife shall remain on Ararat!"

Ham was stunned. Scenes of Shinar flashed to mind, and his lips parted, but no sound came forth.

At last, he managed, "If I refuse?"

"If you refuse, there shall be no bride for Canaan from among your kin."

Ham stared helplessly into the council fire. It seemed a mist had descended over his dreams—impenetrable, irresistible as the cloud that had always darkened his life.

— 8 —

The rickety wagon that had carried Ham's wife and newborn
Canaan to Shinar years ago, and had taken gifts of bride-
price to Noah, was once again traveling through the valley.
This time, Carise rode on the seat next to her second child, Keilah, as
a flop-eared donkey pulled the cart, and the strapping young Canaan
walked eagerly alongside.

Ever since Ham had returned with word that he had procured a
bride, Canaan had been a new person. Joyful, expectant, he no longer
focused unnaturally on his sister, and family life was less strained.

Carise and her daughter wasted no time in preparing to leave
Shinar, as the mother told of life on Ararat and the long-lost clan they
would rejoin.

As for Ham, of course, this was not an easy transition. For his
son's sake, he undertook the move, but only hope that he and a passel
of grandchildren could one day return to the dream of empire kept
his resentments in check.

Still, as they journeyed north, Ham tended to walk far ahead of
his family, not because he was eager to reach Ararat, but because he
preferred a sulking solitude to conversation.

Despite his personal disappointment, Ham had given a glowing
report about the bride-to-be. "Her name is Sherah, daughter of
Japheth," he said. Then, with some gall, he added, " . . . the better of
my two brothers."

Canaan, recalling his father's descriptions of his kin, enthused,
"He is the red-haired one! Does Sherah have red hair?"

The lad, having never seen such a person, could scarcely imagine
anything more strange or more wonderful.

"Yes," Ham said, smiling, "she has a glorious mane of red hair!
She is a bit too fair, if you ask me. But, she is sweet as a flower and
just as dainty."

Carise and Keilah were as enthralled as Canaan, imagining the
joy of female society they would know on the mountan.

When Keilah clapped her hands, exclaiming, "I shall have a grandmother!" Ham's crusty heart could not help but melt a little. Never had it hardened against his mother, and he had to concede to himself that it would be good for his children to be near her.

Even today, as he traipsed ahead of his family, he was conflicted. Sometimes he knew he had been a headstrong fool to turn his back upon his kin.

Still, the past was the past, and it was far from ideal. Canaan had never felt the brunt of his uncles' hatred, and Ham knew there was no way he would escape it.

The past . . .

Like the others of the human remnant who had survived the flood, Ham recalled the lost world with a mix of good and bad memories.

As he sojourned up the valley, he remembered the pristine stretch of land that led from the seaport of Cronos to the vale of Lamechtown, where his grandfather's mill had been.

That area, like all of Adlandia, looked as though it had been laid out by some master landscaper. In the years since the Ark had landed, none of the survivors had grown accustomed to the ongoing tumult that created mountains and scooped out valleys in haphazard wrenchings and twistings of the earth's mantle.

There had been no such thing as "cataclysm" prior to the flood, and, concerning the geography of the earth, it was taken for granted that it was the result of exacting, divine artistry.

Not that "divine" meant the same to everybody.

There was more than one religion on earth, before the Flood. The surviving remnant of humanity were Sethites, descended from the son God had given to Adam and Eve when Cain killed their beloved Abel. The Sethites had kept the traditions of monotheism, worshipping one God, whom they called Yahweh.

The bulk of humanity, however, had worshipped the Sun and a myriad of gods and goddesses, many of whom walked among them and ruled the world of the day. These beings—variously known as the Overlords, the Daemons, the Sons of God—had not only governed humanity, but had taught people how to manipulate nature and the laws of science to recreate the very stuff of life.

They had, in fact, procreated with human women, the result of which were the Nephilim, or the Titans, half-god, half-human beings who had been the military and commanding class, carrying out the will of the gods to the fear and respect of any who would oppose them.

Ham remembered his father's long sermons, the ones Noah gave daily as the crowds had come to Lamechtown to see the notorious "madman" and his famed construction project. For a century the building of the Ark, made of the heaviest of woods and immovable from its inland location, had drawn the attention of scoffing spectators.

God, Noah had proclaimed, would soon destroy the earth with water. None who rejected Yahweh's way of salvation would be spared. To the consternation of his own kin, he had insisted that God's way had nothing to do with tradition, or with human works of "righteousness," but with utter reliance on God, repentance, and faith.

One of the great sins of humanity, he declared, was tampering with the "stuff of life"—the crossbreeding which scientists had performed. The products of this manipulation, countless permutations of species, had so cluttered the population, that it was easy to forget what the original zoological menu had contained. When the technology ventured into mixing animal and human genes, mayhem insued.

Hence, the Ark was built not only to save a human remnant, but as a cargo vessel in which to rescue pairs of each animal species that was part of God's original creation.

To this day, Ham was not certain just why he had been saved from the Flood. His heart had not been knotted to Yahweh for years, but he was one of Noah's sons, and Noah had often told them of God's covenant to save his three offspring and their wives.

It seemed a lifetime ago that the rains had begun, and the horrid volcanic splitting of the planet with its resultant spewing of magma and subterranean founts.

Emboweled in the Ark, the family had not been able to witness the crashing of the sky canopy or the tidal waves that had whipped inland with unimaginable force. But they had heard the cries of lost souls, as they pleaded to enter in, followed by an even more terrible quiet, and then the eruption of all nature.

Even these several years later, Ham sometimes awoke in the middle of the night with memories of those cries and that holocaust.

He had never gotten over the loss of Adlandian civilization, the utter disappearance of its glories and its might.

He longed for more than population, for more than arts and progress. He longed for power, such as the Overlords had possessed and such as those possessed who followed them.

Was it as a warning against such thoughts that the earth suddenly heaved beneath his feet?

With an alert sweep of his eyes, Ham ascertained that the mountains to the west were smoking. One high peak festered with glowing lava, a veritable river of liquid fire tumbling down its side toward the valley.

Carise brought the wagon to a halt and stared open-mouthed at the phenomenon. With agile strength, Canaan grasped the donkey's reins from his mother's hands and pulled him sideways. Fortunately, the creature was not obstinate and responded to the master's urging, sensing that it was in danger.

"Run!" Ham cried, speeding back toward his family. "Head to the east!"

Canaan was already doing just that, as the women, not trusting themselves to the wagon, jumped down and ran beside him.

Leaping rocks and bushes upon the alluvial plain, the family and its long-eared charge fled the distant eruption. They had seen volcanoes before and knew that the molten river, though miles away, could take only minutes to cross the intervening expanse.

Already a great cloud of ash darkened the sky, spreading out across the valley like a death mantle. The temperature of the pleasant day was rising quickly as the ash, though blocking the sun, pressed in upon the earth with its own heat.

Soon it would be dark as night, as the ash fell to the ground, filtering all light from the sky.

With a sound like rockets, a sound reminiscent of the military machines of lost Adlandia, huge plugs of rock and lava shot upward from the volcano's spout.

The family, dodging falling debris, picked their way through the unnatural dusk.

In the gloaming of the eastern mountains, close to the river, it appeared there was a bushy swale. Ham hastened his family toward it, hoping the lava missiles would not reach so far.

On cut and bleeding feet, the fearful little group made their way to the grotto's meager shelter. Here palms and date trees surrounded a moist hollow, and the family ducked inside, huddling together and peering between the spindly trunks toward the fiery western skyline.

Hours passed, until the volcanic darkness was indistinguishable from actual night.

Ham drew his loved ones into a protective embrace. With each whistling eruption, the women trembled, Keilah burying her face on her father's broad shoulder.

But of the four, it was Canaan who was most distressed, not for fear of the elements, so much, as wondering if he was truly meant to gain the slopes of Ararat.

— 9 —

Morning brought hope. The volcanic activity had subsided, and the sun was actually breaking through the ash, enough of which had fallen to the ground that the family could breathe without covering their noses.

Emerging from the grove, Ham led his family forth, and the two women climbed atop the wagon seat once again.

But not before Carise, with the same concern for the donkey that she had always exhibited toward the animals on the Ark, wiped the doltish creature's eyes with a corner of her shawl. A fine black soot came off on the cloth, caked with sleep.

"There, there," she crooned to the donkey, "now you can see to take us to our long-lost people."

As she stroked the animal's ears, Ham looked on fondly. "Your mother was the best caretaker a zoo ever had," Ham told the children. "When we were on the Ark, she used to exercise the animals every day."

"How did she do that?" Keilah marveled. "Was there room?"

"There were open spaces on each deck," Ham said. "And the upper deck was her race track and her arena, protected from the rains by a huge roof. I will never forget seeing her trot back and forth with the giraffes and tug on the lazy lions as though they were pets!"

"Now, Ham," Carise interjected, "things were different with the animals in those days. They had no fear of us. It was as though God changed their dispositions for that special time."

"Possibly," Ham said. "But you will admit you have always had a way with wild things."

"I suppose," Carise conceded. "After all, I have a way with you."

At this, the family laughed, and some of the tension of the night dissipated.

As though in response to their conversation, however, the air was suddenly rent by a pathetic cry. Long and low, it seemed to come from alongside the river, just to the east.

Carise's sympathetic heart was pricked, and the four humans scanned the bank, wondering what might be the source of the trouble.

"Look!" Canaan gasped. "There is a bog. Something might have fallen in."

As he took off to investigate, Ham cautioned him. "Be careful, son. If an animal is caught there, it could be too afraid to let you help."

The people who had come from the Ark had more than once seen such situations in the new world. Animals did not have an easy time of it in the unstable terrain. Earthquakes had claimed many an unwary beast in sudden rifts of the ground's crust; strange tar pits dotted the landscape and sink holes full of wet sand had sucked others to their deaths.

In the years since the Ark had touched ground, the beastly cargo had multiplied magnificently, but it was always a sad thing to witness the very ones who had survived the flood, or their near offspring, meeting untimely ends in the still-forming terrain.

As Canaan approached the bog, one of thousands that lay along the low banks of new rivers, the gutteral sounds of a desperate creature were joined by other, even more plaintive, cries.

"It is a tiger!" Canaan called over his shoulder. "And her cub is with her!"

Emitting a cry of her own, Carise took out across the field, followed close behind by Keilah and Ham.

What the onlookers found was heart wrenching. A great striped beast, her coat drenched with swampy ooze, flailed helplessly in the dank puddle, her very movements speeding the certainty of her doom.

With each desperate slapping of her huge feet upon the murky surface, she slipped further down, while her cub, a fluff of white and black streaks, watched helplessly from the pond's edge, its squeals only spurring the mother's frantic efforts.

"I know this cat!" Carise groaned. "I called her Mandela! I used to walk her every day on the Ark!"

In horror, the woman looked on as the beast, who had once been like a pet to her, struggled for its last breaths.

Ham tried to pull his wife away, but Carise would not comply. "Oh, husband!" she wailed. "Is there nothing we can do?"

The man's silence was answer enough. He was, however, able to turn her away before the cat took its final desperate gasp and sank for the last time beneath the muck.

Keilah sat sadly upon the ground, and Carise fell to her knees, weeping disconsolately.

Only Canaan saw that something could be done.

Racing to the edge of the bog, he reached for the cub, who tottered precariously on the brink, thinking to join its mother.

"Here, little fellow," he said. "Mama is gone now."

Lifting the cub to his chest, he cradled it in strong arms and ran his fingers through its kittenish fur.

Then, turning back toward the family, he brought it to Carise. Tenderly, he laid the distraught creature on the woman's lap.

"You can name this one Mandela, too," he suggested. "It is the picture of its mother."

For years to come, Carise would never be seen without the company of that proud white tiger. A descendant of the Ark's cargo, the cat, like so much on earth, was a reminder that life always renews itself.

—10—

awn broke over Ararat, lighting up the Ark's mountain like the first sunrise of the new world. Canaan crept forth from the wedding tent where his new bride slept, and basked in the sun's rays.

He scanned the common that linked the three small dwellings of his uncles and grandfather, and lingered over the meeting hall where just last evening he had taken Sherah to wife.

He had not slept all night.

His young heart was too full for sleep. It seemed every hope he had ever hoped and every dream he had ever dreamed was coming to pass. Excitement for life overwhelmed him.

Behind, in the tent, was surely the most lovely creature God had ever placed on Earth, before or since the Great Flood. Slender as the gazelles that ranged the Shinar plain, pretty as a scarlet poppy. . .

In truth, Sherah and her sisters were the only girls, besides Keilah, on whom he had ever laid eyes. Yet, his bride would have won his heart just as easily had he chosen her from among thousands.

And how quickly it had all happened! One day, a lonely boy upon the Tigris fields, hopeless as a stranded buck—the next, on his way to the mountain from which all life and hope had sprung.

Suddenly, he was a husband, possibly soon a father. . .

He reached for the mantle tied about his naked waist and drew it over his shoulders with quivering fingers. The prospect was challenging.

As was everything about Ararat.

Canaan was ready for it all. He had learned what Ham had to offer. Yet he had long sensed that the goals of empire and conquest were but a part of greatness.

He did not know, just now, of what other things greatness might consist. But he was eager to learn and sensed that the answers lay with Noah.

Reverence for his grandfather had been instilled at his mother's knee—on dark evenings when she and he and his little sister had sat

52

beside the cave fire all alone. It had been ingrained before he ever dreamed of meeting the patriarch, on long afternoons when Ham had gone hunting and Carise told naptime tales of the Ark, of Adlandia, and of the gods whom Noah had outshone.

From those early, well-planted seeds had sprung a spiritual bent, a longing to pursue deeper and deeper things.

At times, the isolation of his growing-up years had strangled him, the sprouting urges of young manhood nearly tearing him from the ways he wished to trust.

Of all things mortal, he had longed for Ham's approval; he received it in great gulps, only to feel it cool when he asked questions.

Now, here they all were—Ham, Carise, Keilah, Noah, Shem, and Japheth—sharing the mountain together . . . something which he had been told could never happen.

The name of God was still uneasy on Canaan's lips. He had heard it often from his mother, but had never used the term in manly conversation. Now he longed to sit with the elders about the council fire, to listen to his uncles and his grandfather as they spoke of the Almighty.

Furtively, he uttered Yahweh's name in whispered prayer, his soul burgeoning with zeal for the future.

Dawn filled the Ararat vale with a sudden blush, and Canaan turned his eyes toward the Ark. For a long while, he sat studying it, until his bride roused from slumber and, finding him gone, pulled back the tent flap.

Though she was very young and very innocent, the wedding night had bound her to the dusky son of Shinar, unfettering emotions she had never known lay dormant within her.

At the sight of him sitting in the early light, his dark head raised heavenward, she feared to call his name. Yet she need not have feared. He was attuned to her like the seasons to the sun, and at her slightest movement, he turned to draw her out.

"Come . . . ." he whispered, almost afraid to break the rosy twilight, "sit beside me . . ."

"Husband . . . ." she pleaded, shaking her head and holding forth a beckoning hand.

A ready smile lit his countenance, and he jumped to fulfill her request.

Crawling back into the tent, he buried his face in her neck. With gentle strokes, she ran her fingers through his tousled hair and pressed herself against him.

They were both teacher and pupil to each other, unschooled but artful as roebuck and doe, following the inclinations of their hearts and the strange pulse that pulled them on.

Canaan had come home—to Ararat, to Yahweh, and to love.

—11—

When the time for the afternoon rest had come, and when the elders of the camp had found places of shade in which to recline, Canaan sought out his grandfather.

Taking Sherah by the hand, the groom led her to Noah's cottage, where they discovered him sitting in the cool of the doorway.

Because Canaan was in awe of the aging patriarch, and because he did not know him well, he bowed low upon seeing him, and spoke in measured tones, "My wife and I have a request."

Sherah, who had grown up in Noah's presence, and who was as close to him as to her own father, observed Canaan's reverence with a twinkle in her eye.

She remembered her mother's horror when it was announced that the son of Ham would be her groom. She recalled her own fear at the prospect. After all, Japheth taught her that the seed of Ham was evil and that it was best they lived far away.

Noah had not preached this. But Sherah noticed that sadness marked her grandfather's face whenever Ham's name was mentioned—a sadness tinged with longing which she had never understood.

She understood well enough now. Canaan was *not* evil. He was, she believed, the kindest of men. As his bride, she reasoned, she should be the best judge of that.

The patriarch, struck by Canaan's polite approach, bid the couple join him on the doorstep. He knew Canaan less than Sherah did. But, like the bride, he admired the quiet young man arisen from the mists of Hiddekel.

"What is your petition?" Noah inquired, studying the handsome lad with pride.

Canaan would not mince words. "To see the Ark," he replied, "and to board her."

Noah glanced at Sherah in surprise. "Such a request is simple enough. But, your bride has entered the vessel many times."

Sherah shrugged. "I have never seen it with Canaan," she deferred.

"Yes," the youngster urged him. "Is it not a holy thing, which a man and wife should share?"

This matter-of-fact statement revealed Canaan's character more clearly than anything else he could have said. Never had Noah dreamed the son of Ham possessed such yearnings.

His old eyes sparkling, the patriarch reached forth and embraced Canaan's sturdy shoulders. "The hike would do me good," he said.

• • •

Slowly the three ascended the mount. As they approached the great monolith of history, where it hung out from the landing place like a black and fearsome fortress, Canaan's heart pounded. The closer they came, the more he sensed time reversing, as though he stepped through the portal of a previous world.

"*You* built this vessel, Grandfather?" he marveled.

"Yes—I and my father, Lamech, and my brother, Jaseth." The elder's voice was husky at the remembrance of those departed ones. Canaan could not know the depth of his sadness at the memory, not only of the godly Lamech, but of the brother who had been lost with the unbelievers.

"What was it like," Canaan mused, "to construct such a ship? Did it take many years, Grandfather?"

Noah chuckled, thumping the earth with his walking stick. "A century, to be exact," he asserted. "And all the while, people laughed at us."

Canaan was pricked by this. "They were destroyed," he recalled.

"Yes," Noah replied gravely. "All but my own small family." Then, peering sideways at Canaan, he said, "Someone has taught you this. Your mother, I suppose?"

"Indeed!" Canaan answered. "She taught me much—of the world as it was, of the animals, and of the mighty works of Adlandia—of the Overlords and their evil designs!"

Noah nodded. "This is good," he said. "She has done well by you." Then, wistfully, "Did Ham teach you, also?"

Canaan looked away. "I often asked him questions, but he rarely had time for answers."

When they reached the runway, leading to the vessel's gopher-wood door, Canaan surveyed the mammoth sweep of timber, his eyes wide with amazement.

Noah stepped to the door and placed a reverent hand on the lever. With a creak and a groan, the portal opened, and Noah turned to the children with a smile.

"Come," he bade.

Canaan took his bride's hand, as much for comfort as for love. Stepping beneath the lintel, the lad coughed, as the musty smell of ancient fodder and dusty cobwebs greeted him.

Inside, the three waited for their eyes to adjust to the shadows. Once they did, a narrow ladder could be seen.

"Careful," Noah warned. "It is rickety."

The old man seemed infused with energy as he entered the Ark. As though time had turned back, he took on the air of captain and master.

"We will begin on the top deck," he announced, directing them upstairs. "Stalls and cages are there, and a court where Carise used to exercise the creatures."

Together they laughed, Canaan having recently heard these stories, and Noah envisioning them.

"There is so much I need to know," declared Canaan. "Is it true that it never rained before the Flood? Was the sky white? Were there evil beings in the cities? Could people fly? Was the Earth as wicked as mother says?"

Noah's expression was wistful. Taking Canaan by the arm, he slowed him down.

"There, there," he said, "all in good time. Let's see now—where shall I start?"

Hours they would stay within the ship that day, wandering up and down and through her, Noah talking all the while, as he had not talked for years, of things past and mysteries shrouded by time.

—12—

The week following Canaan's marriage, he and his bride moved from the bridal tent at the center of the village to take up residence with Sherah's father. The fact that Canaan would dwell with Japheth did not mean, however, that he had won the man's approval, or that he had become an accepted member of Ararat society.

His presence would be tolerated because Father Noah wished it. But Canaan's way would be hard upon the mountain.

The lad, who had entered the region starry-eyed with expectation, learned all too quickly what a cold place the world could be.

Though he had grown up oblivious to the "curse," it did not take long for him to deduce his awful position once he entered Ararat vale. The shame was whispered behind his back too often; it glinted in hate-filled eyes. It was intimated by a dozen wagging tongues, and finally, one stormy night, it was spoken outright at the council fire.

Noah was not present in the longhouse that evening, but the lad was thrilled just to be in the same room with his uncles—men who guarded the oracles of God. The son of Ham listened eagerly as they expounded the history of the human race.

As they discoursed on the tale of Cain and Abel, the young groom was spellbound, for this version was one he had never heard before.

Enthralled, he watched the elders' fiery countenances as they recited the ancient legend, their rhythmic cadences matching peals of thunder and the raging of the elements beyond the chamber walls. "Murder," "jealousy," "exile"—the words fashioned in deep drama filled the smoky air with a hundred vivid images.

Sometimes, to Canaan's surprise, when Abel's murdering brother was mentioned, eyes glanced toward Ham, who stared somberly into the flames.

"Why do you look at my father?" Canaan wished to ask.

But he did not voice the question, listening quietly to his uncles' conclusions. As he did so, the folk legend took on a horrifying dimension.

"Cursed, Cain was," Shem was saying, "as Ham also has been."

At this, Canaan leaned forth, studying Shem incredulously. Fearing to break the recitation's spell, he spoke up nonetheless, his tone imbued with respect. "Good uncle," he interrupted, "perhaps our forefather was *'cursed,'* as you contend. But what great sin has my father committed that you should compare him with . . . a murderer?"

Japheth leered at Ham, who glanced away uneasily. So, Ham had never told Canaan of the crime committed the very night of his birth! He had never recounted the great indignity he had perpetrated upon Noah when he found him drunk and naked in the tent.

As Shem, with some enjoyment, set the matter forth in grisly detail, Canaan's expression lost its eager spark. "Some are *as the night to shadows,"* the elder summarized. "Ham is one of these."

Canaan's mind sped with a thousand tumults. How he wished Noah were here! Surely he would have brought some balance to the tale. And Ham—why did he not defend himself?

But before the youngster could plead for further illumination, Japheth cinched the bond of guilt even closer, and the lad felt a sinking in his soul, as if the maw of ruin gaped beneath him.

"'Cursed be Canaan,'" Japheth recited. "'A servant of servants shall he be to this brethren.'"

With this, silence overtook the longhouse, only the licking fire and pounding rain interrupting. Canaan turned desperate eyes to his father, hoping against hope that he would cast the story in a different light.

But Ham's only response was to stand on shaky legs, not daring to look his son in the face, and exit the room without a word.

—13—

From the day Canaan learned of the curse, he kept his questions to himself, doing his duties, loving his wife. As the months went on, however, he found that he must struggle for any fragment of respect his brethren parceled out, and even his own father avoided him.

Ham had returned to Ararat to please Carise, to find a bride for Canaan, and not to find his destiny upon its slopes. With time, the resentment he felt toward Noah became resentment toward his son.

After all, he would still be in Shinar if it had not been for the boy. Furthermore, despite his uncles' intolerance, Canaan seemed pleased to dwell in the tabernacles of Shem and Japheth, to learn the ways of Noah and all the old traditions. With each passing month, Ham's hopes that the lad would follow his dreams of a Hamite kingdom were further from grasp.

So the young man, who had come here wanting to pursue the ways of God, found more and more obstacles raised against himself.

When, shortly after the boy's marriage, Carise blessed Ham with a second son, Canaan found his position more alien than ever.

Carise had accompanied her husband to Ararat in accordance with Noah's stipulation, understanding that if they were ever to leave again, Canaan must stay on the mountain. When she found herself with child, she rejoiced, believing that life for her in the Ararat community was forever established. What she did not know was that this second child would force her into a more lonely condition than she had ever known.

As the second son grew, he was tall and darle like the firstborn, but took after his father in more ways than Canaan had.

Cush was his name. Ham had chosen it to instill his ongoing hopes within the child, for the word meant "black," and Ham saw in his new son a portent of great things.

Canaan had failed him, he reasoned. But Cush would not. If the firstborn had spurned his heritage, the second would redeem it.

60

It was at the longhouse, eight days after Carise had delivered the newborn, that Canaan first laid eyes upon him. Noah had called for the babe's circumcision to be performed, according to tradition, upon that day. All the Ararat males were present, and all but Canaan had received the mark at some time in their lives.

Canaan had left his mother outside the door with the other women of camp, where she would anxiously await the conclusion of the ordeal. Entering the room with Ham, Canaan stood nearby as the man of Shinar placed the swaddled babe upon Noah's outstretched hands.

The day of Cush's birth, Ham had lifted him skyward, invoking the blessing of whatever vague deity he served and endowing him with his unique name. Today, Noah would see to it that the One True God received the lad, and that the seal of Yahweh abided in the child's very flesh.

Laying the little one upon a stone slab in the midst of the company, Noah drew out a flint knife and pulled back the rough blanket in which the child was wrapped, revealing to his brethren the health and wholeness of Yahweh's handiwork. Then, with a dexterous flash of the sharp instrument, he removed the infant's foreskin, calling out above the babe's offended squall the blessing of God Almighty.

Canaan, who had never before witnessed the ceremony, was moved by it, wondering at the import, which was not explained to him, and also wondering if his uninitiated status might ever be corrected. The day he saw his little brother receive the mark, he was impressed as never before with just how alien he was.

To be sure, Ham had brought Cush to the longhouse out of compulsion, and not out of a willing heart. Because of his falling-out with Noah the night of Canaan's birth, he had never been compelled to submit his firstborn to the knife, and would not have allowed Cush the "shame" had he, not now been subject to the old traditions.

Canaan easily read his father's resentment of the rite. As soon as it had been performed, the man reached for the babe, drawing the swaddling clothes over his bleeding groin and carrying him quickly into the open air.

Pushing past Carise, who waited outside, he hastened down the mountain toward home. When he entered his house, he shut the door firmly behind him and did not bring the child forth for many days.

From that hour, whenever Canaan encountered Cush in the fields, the village byways, or at family gatherings, he watched him closely. If the seal of Yahweh ensured success, Cush would surely have it.

And with the years that followed, it appeared Cush was, of all men, most successful.

— INTERLUDE —

Old King Melchizedek, the master storyteller, leaned back in his cedar chair and called for a cup of wine.

Ali, his servant boy, quickly fetched the carafe and poured a gobletful. All evening he had sat with the king, enchanted by his tale and not at all sleepy.

Melchizedek, likewise, seemed full of energy, as though the recitation had infused him with new life.

"Sir," said the lad, his dark eyes snapping, "the plot deepens now. Cush and Canaan will be rivals, right?"

The king winked and raised a gnarled finger.

"You are perceptive, child. But they shall be more than rivals."

"Enemies, then!" declared the boy.

"They shall teach their own sons very differently," Melchizedek nodded. "And in the sons, the future lies."

Even at his young age, the boy understood the wisdom of this.

"*How* will they be different, Master?" Ali inquired. "Will they be so different that they go to war?"

This was said with such youthful enthusiasm, Melchizedek shuddered.

"War, war!" he muttered. "Does even *your* blood thrill to the notion?"

Ali sat back, red-faced, and Melchizedek cleared his throat, casting his gaze again out the eastward window.

"Indeed," he sighed wistfully, "I suppose war was inevitable. But first, the hatred must flower . . ."

PART II

"And Cush begat Nimrod: he began to be a mighty one in the earth. He was a mighty hunter before the Lord: wherefore it is said, Even as Nimrod the mighty hunter before the Lord."

—Genesis 10:8,9

"Melchizedek, the son of Canaan, whom God had chosen from all generations of men . . ."

—Ethiopian Book of Adam and Eve 3:13ff
(Lore and Tradition)

The Two Kings

—14—

As the families of Ararat grew, so did their range of activity, until three separate centers emerged. At first they were no more than widely dispersed dwellings, the smaller stone cottages being abandoned as the sons' children spread down the mountain, as larger garden and grazing areas were marked off for each group, and as the great-grandchildren came along.

Noah maintained his two-room residence nearest the Ark, and developed beside it a famed grape arbor, known for the fine wines it produced. Never since the night of Canaan's birth had he fallen prey to drunkenness, and never again would he. But his descendants may have intended a good-natured tease when they changed the name of their grandfather's little village from Heshton ("the eight survivors") to Aghurri or Ahora, meaning "he planted the vine."

Shem's part of the mountain remained close to his father's, and lay on the northeast face.

Sedeqetelebab he named it, for his wife, the "righteous of heart." This designation, however, could have been a play on words. For, the term could also be translated "hill of the golden woman," and could have referred to Sindra's golden hair, of which Shem had always been proud.

On the west side of the mountain lay the village of Japheth, which, some said, he, too, had named for his wife. Others maintained it referred to the first bride of the new world, his daughter, Sherah. Canaan, who worked its fields day in and day out, liked to think the latter was true, for Adataneses, meaning "the daintiness of women," or "the daintiness of joy," certainly fit the girl, who was delicate as a reed and a joy to behold.

Finally, there was the town of Ham, farthest south on the Ararat plain. But, there was neither humor nor joy in the name Ham gave the place. Naeltamauk, "inheritance of the disinherited," was a constant reminder of the irreparable rift between himself and Noah.

The aging patriarch could not win out over it, and with each new generation of children, the chasm seemed broader.

Even the mountain began to be parceled up, as though one name could not contain it all.

While Noah had often called the height on which the Ark rested Mount Judi, meaning "Mountain of Praise," God's saving hand was not always foremost in others' thinking. As the family spread across the foothills, it became necessary to distinguish the various humps of one great range. Hence, the resting place of the Ark was designated Mount Lubar of the Ararats, meaning "Mountain of the Ship." Or when people wanted to specify its locale, they described the area as Mount Masu, meaning "Twin Peaks," for the ship rested in a saddle, between two high points.

Every other rise along the precipitous horizon was given a separate label, every pocket and valley a special name.

For mankind was still the segregator, the cataloger, and the divider of things. His territories spoke his heart, as much as did the harsh words of his lips.

• • •

While the mountain society developed, Cush's potential commanded attention. Ham recognized early that the boy would be a master huntsman, a skilled tracker, and that he had inherited Tubal-Cain's talent for fashioning weapons and knives.

When the pockets and caves of the Ararat range yielded their lodes of gold, iron, copper, and coal, the burgeoning society that had spread into a hundred nooks and crannies was catapulted past the simple life. No longer was every man a hunter, a farmer, or a herdsman, only. Crafts and arts attracted a following.

Cush was one of the first to hear the artisan's call. He was greatly sought after for his facility with hammer, tong, and anvil.

He was, in fact, a multitalented fellow—fulfilling his father's love of sport and game, the tribal dream of fame and prosperity, and the urge to create those things which, on Earth, represented security.

Not so, Canaan. Today, as he worked the soil of Japheth's little farm, he cast weary eyes north toward the Ark. In the sunset light that reflected through westerly rain clouds, the old ship seemed a little stooped, as if it, too, were weary.

The young toiler wiped sweat from his brow and sighed, leaning upon his crudely fashioned hoe. Sometimes, when he peered down the tunnel of his future, it seemed there was no light, only mindless drudgery that would culminate in the grave. Resentment and jealousy threatened to strangle the desire for things sublime.

But when he considered the aging vessel, he remembered the shadows and dusky smells of the ship's interior, as he had experienced them the day Noah gave him the tour. That day, the very substance of the Ark had assured him of God's love.

Ghosts of divine promises still stalked the corridors of the mighty sentinel, and despite its venerable age, it symbolized hope.

Surely God had not abandoned Canaan. Stooped or not, the Ark was a reminder of that truth.

Digging his hoe into the soil, Canaan practiced gratitude, a trait that required as much nurturing as the garden he tilled.

Were he to neglect it, it could be choked by weeds of self-pity, or crushed by thistles of hate.

—15—

C ush stood in the hollow beyond his private dwelling observing the workers of his enormous limestone kiln, one of the many instruments of industry that had thrived beneath his management.

Even at this distance, fifty feet from the brick oven, the heat was intense as it radiated from the red-hot interior. Close to the kiln's sides, the blast was nearly unbearable. The workmen who stoked it were paid well for their discomfort and were allowed frequent shift changes, during which they could bathe in a shaded pool nearby.

Lime, carted miles from a mountain quarry, was burned to a powder within the oven—hundreds of pounds being processed per day. When mixed with liquid from the tumbling headwaters of the Tigris, which flowed not far distant, the substance made a fine cement.

With this miracle of mortar, along with the smelting of metal made possible by coal fuel, men dared to believe that civilization could flourish once again.

Memories of Adlandia had never died. As long as there were those on Earth who had experienced the wonders of the pre-Flood world, there would be the goal of reconstructing its marvels. Even once that generation had passed away, tales of that great age would produce undying dreams of progress.

Architecture, especially in the domain of Ham and Cush, was already far beyond the primitive. Cush surveyed the meeting hall that graced his own village, and a gleam flashed through his eyes. Its formal symmetry, emphasized in evenly spaced pilasters, made the longhouse of Noah's little town an embarrassment. The columns, designed to resemble those of Adlandia's legendary temples, loomed nearly fifteen feet up from an ample porch, which was paved in shining terrazzo tiles. Walls of well-polished stone, minutely mortared along fine seams, were enhanced here and there with carvings of godlike faces and heroic scenes.

While Ham denied that the building and its decorative features were inspired by pagan deities, Cush did not much care what their origin was. The simple glory of the structure was a joy.

Afternoon sunlight glinted across the multihued porch, which, like all Hamitic buildings, faced south, toward Shinar. The colonnade, paved in a rare salmon-colored limestone, was embedded with a mosaic of white marble chips, as reminiscent of seashell pearl as anything in this landlocked region could be.

People did not know where the oceans of the new world lay. There was no sea visible from even the highest points of the Ararat range. But the legends of Adlandia's maritime peoples persisted, and always the desire burned in the human breast to return to great waters, along which the most advanced societies of the earlier continent had flourished.

Cush dreamed of one day finding the sea. But his hopes also lingered over the snowy heights of the interior land mass. According to tales rehearsed around his father's fire, that had been the home of the highest Overlords—the caste of gods and demigods that once ruled the planet.

Ham's theology, while an enigma to his sons, was laced with enough references to these beings that neither Canaan nor Cush were ignorant of the important role the Guardians had played in past times. Though Cush was not deeply spiritual, he sometimes wondered what had become of the strange Watchers who dominated the world of Noah's time.

Today, smoke from the kiln wafted northward, carrying his mind past material things to the slopes of the distant highlands. Clouds always covered the silent peaks, and he wondered if they shrouded more than rock and ice.

—16—

When Sherah, Canaan's wife, brought forth her firstborn, Sidon, it was in the spring of the year following Cush's birth. Hence, though the two children were of different generations, one being nephew to the other, they were so close in age as to be continually compared.

Perhaps because of the oppressed status into which Sidon was born, wanderlust overtook him early on. He was in love with the fields and hills of Ararat, distressing his parents with amblings far from home. He was especially impressed by tales of the sea and its commerce in ancient times.

Sidon, the Dreamer, people called him. "See how useless he is, while Cush thrives on industry."

Canaan, who knew how it felt to compete with Cush, feared that his son had inherited the "curse." Though he saw to it that the boy was circumcised on the eighth day after birth, just as Cush had been, there appeared little hope that the child would ever succeed in Ararat society.

While Cush was a "son of Ham," he had gained respect through his talents and his wealth. He did not bear the brunt of Ham's outcast position. Sidon, on the other hand, showed no creative genius that would earn esteem.

Nor did he care to. The life of far-flung travel left little time for such concerns.

What Canaan knew of God, he tried to share with Sidon. But the lad never sat still for catechism.

One day, after working all afternoon with his father on Japheth's farm, he began to itch for adventure. Canaan had seen it coming, the urge for travel that frequently sparked through the boy's eyes. It did not surprise him, therefore, when the lad did not show up at supper.

As Canaan entered the house, he found Sherah, bent over a simmering stewpot, trying to hide her tear-smudged face.

"I do not blame the boy," she wept. "Nor would I blame you, husband, if *you* left home. Japheth keeps both of you bound to drudgery.

Every day I see you, toiling on his land, having received no place of your own from your father or from mine . . . How do you bear it?"

Canaan resisted the truth so plainly spoken. The facts of their condition had rarely passed in words between them, and the man cringed to hear it laid out.

Suddenly, fist clenched, he left the low stone building that he had shared with his bride since the week of their wedding. Sherah, following him to the door, wondered at his strange demeanor.

But as she watched him glare stormily up the mountain and then depart into the gloaming of its slopes, she did not call him back. She knew he wished to be alone, and that the shadow of the Ark was always a solace.

● ● ●

Canaan ascended the plank leading to the Ark's high doorway and seated himself on the threshold, drawing his knees to his chin and clasping his legs close to his body. For a long time he buried his face in his lap and waited for night to descend.

Away down the valley were the campfires and house lights of his many relatives, flickering like fireflies as far south as he could see.

South . . . the land of Shinar. For the first time since coming here, he wished he had stayed in that primeval country.

For years the burning hope that he might find, upon these slopes, the very meaning of life, had buoyed him above ridicule and intolerance. "Ham's curse" had never conquered him, as the joy of knowing Noah, of dwelling on the holy site where the rainbow had touched down, bolstered his faith and encouraged his longing spirit.

He was willing to devote himself to Japheth, to take the role of a servant, to always be quiet in Shem's shadow, if it meant he could learn from all they had to teach.

But what hope was there, if even his own son spurned his deepest yearnings? Perhaps, indeed, the line of Canaan would never amount to anything, on either the human or spiritual level. Perhaps, truly, Yahweh despised Ham's firstborn from the day of his birth, and Canaan would bear his father's sin for all time.

As he sat on the Ark's narrow porch, moonlight spread across the valley, casting a pall of despair over his heart. No—he was not too proud to serve his brothers, nor to lay down his life for Yahweh. But he must have hope, or he would surely die.

—17—

With dawn's grey light, a tremor at the bottom of the plank awoke Canaan, who had fallen asleep in the high doorway. Rubbing his swollen eyes, he peered down the runway and saw that his grandfather, Noah, was ascending the narrow board.

"Canaan," the old man called, a smile gilding his voice, "what brings you here at so early an hour?"

"Not so early," the younger replied. "I have been here since last evening."

"Ah," Noah said with a nod. "Then you meant this visit for meditation."

"I suppose," Canaan said wistfully, as the patriarch sat down beside him.

Noah could not miss the tone of weary despair that marked the lad's words. Studying him carefully, he whispered, "Where does the pain reside, my son?"

"Here . . ." Canaan answered, placing his fist to his breast, his lips quivering.

Noah drew him close, wrapping a fatherly arm about his shoulders. He said nothing, letting the silence draw the sorrow out.

At last, Canaan sighed heavily. "Is it true, Grandfather, that some men are damned before they are born?"

Noah kept his eyes to the far horizon, and without a blink asked, "Who has told you this?"

"It is something I have concluded . . . from the teachings of my uncles."

The patriarch registered no surprise. It was his turn, now, to heave a sigh. "They have doubtless spoken of the 'curse'; is this correct?" he inquired.

"Years ago they did so . . ."

Noah looked at his grandson in wonder. "All this time you have carried the burden of their cruelty, and you have not come to me? I

74

can imagine the twist they put upon the prophecy! Why did you not speak with me regarding this?"

Canaan shrugged out from Noah's embrace. "So, it *was* a prophecy! What hope can any man have against a *prophecy*? And what could you have told me to soften its blow?"

Noah, marking his grandson's desperation, answered the challenge softly. "Do you think I have not agonized over the words I uttered the day Ham left Ararat? They have been a barb to my soul, just as they are to yours and his. Yes, my son, they *are* a barb for your father, as much as he may try to conceal it."

Canaan glanced toward Ham's distant village, his heart aching.

"But," Noah continued, "they were not my words alone. They were the words of Yahweh, an indelible truth. Nonetheless," he went on, "all my years with the Ark have shown me that God does not see as man sees, and man does not hear the words of God with a pure heart. I have come to know, in my spirit, that though your way is hard upon Earth, and though you bear the torment of your father's iniquity, the fruit of that torment shall be atonement."

Canaan had been respectful to this point. He could comprehend the idea of consequences, of inescapable cause and effect. But to couple the notion with atonement was repugnant.

"*I* must atone . . . for my *father's* guilt?" he cried. "I repudiate the very thought!"

Quickly the patriarch intervened between his beloved grandson and such heresy. "No, lad, neither you nor any other man is capable of such expiation. I did not mean that *you* would make atonement, but that the fruit of your suffering would, in time, yield salvation."

Canaan shook his head. "Forgive me, Grandfather," he grimaced, "but such language is, to me, mere double-talk. Oh, I have tried to find light for my path, salvation for my feet. I have reasoned that because I was raised a child of Shinar, because my father sinned, because I was denied the oracles or the mark of circumcision, perhaps I deserve nothing. Yet, my heart is bound to Yahweh, in all my ignorance. Would that I could pluck from my breast the love I feel toward the Almighty!" He shuddered. "He is a cruel and heartless God, damning those who seek Him, and favoring those who have been privileged to know Him from their first breath!"

Tears rose to Noah's eyes, and his throat went dry. "Don't you see?" the grandfather managed. "You are, of all men, close to Yahweh. I knew it from the day we toured the Ark together. No, my son, it is not the color of a man's skin or the place of a man's birth that endears him to the Lord. It is not the might of his achievements, or the oracles to which he is privy, or the ancestry which he bears in his blood. Man honors such things, but God looks upon the heart. And, you shall never escape your love of things high and holy, nor the destiny of greatness that lies before you."

By now, Canaan was weeping sorely. He could not bear another word. "If only I could believe you, Grandfather!" he pleaded. "I have tried to raise Sidon in the fear of the Lord, but he spurns the path of God. Where is the hope for my descendants if they reject even *my* feeble teachings?"

The questions hung uncomfortably between the prophet and his beloved, until the dim light of a distant glory flooded Noah's aged face.

"A priesthood . . . a righteous king . . ." he whispered.

"What?" Canaan was uncertain he had heard correctly.

"A king of righteousness shall be your seed, my son. A priest of God Almighty. . . ."

The youngster was incredulous. As sunlight illumined the Ark's weathered shell, Canaan leaned against the doorpost in silent wonder. He would have asked more questions, but he had no words to frame them.

—18—

J ust as wanderlust had overtaken Sidon, so the lust for greater and greater glory consumed Cush. His inclinations were no sorrow to Ham, who encouraged them as evidence of his own hopes and dreams.

Father and son, together, were accomplishing wonders. Each year their industries and their technologies evolved at a faster rate. Mining and smelting sent dust and smoke into the thin air and up the ridges of Ararat. Complex irrigation systems and roadways began to link field with field and village with village across the populated miles of the valley, and some began to look upon Ham's special condition in a different light.

Indeed, the "curse" was Canaan's, not Cush's. And if the father of them both had been outcast, his uniqueness was deemed stardom among certain folk. In clusters they attached themselves to the elite Hamitic strain.

Commerce on the mountain became increasingly dependent upon the southern quarter. Progress sprang from that region, and there Cush began to develop the first full-fledged cities, until the area closest to the Ark—the quaint townships of Japheth, Shem and Noah—were known as the outback.

Any man endowed with a talent could find a niche in Ham's society. If he was gifted physically, he could find more than enough manual labor to fill his days and his purse. If he had a mind for numbers and for measures, he could turn it to the science of engineering. If he possessed an artistic bent, or a draftsman's eye, he could be an architect.

As the years passed, as the urge for rudimentary building was satisfied, and as people's stomachs were always full, still finer pursuits were indulged, until music, sculpture, carving, and poetry were specialized and honored professions.

All of this took decades to unfold, but in the scheme of history and the experience of that era, it was a mere breath of time. Since men's lifespans encompassed the advent of several generations, folks lived to see it all develop within their appointed days on Earth.

Likewise, since a man might easily live five hundred years, and since if a soul died before reaching his three-hundredth birthday he was said to have died a child, people bore dozens of sons and daughters during their lifetimes. Hence, the population grew, not generationally, but geometrically. An explosion in numbers!

In droves they settled near Ham's estate, looking to him and to Cush for their direction.

Gradually, the old oracles were replaced by new ones. Since neither Ham nor his second-born were heartbound to Yahweh, their followers were fertile soil for a hundred seeds of error.

Noah's voice could not be heard above Cush's seductive song. The second son of Ham, whose eyes lingered over the mysteries of the clouds, would give names to his own illusions.

Though no Overlords walked the Earth, or communed with humankind as in the days of old, their legends still stirred men's imaginations.

The gods would one day return, Cush claimed, and he would win their favors for himself!

—19—

C anaan's plow struck an obstinate rock in his father-in-law's maize plot. Stifling a curse, he bent over to dislodge it, his back aching from the day's labor.

Conquest and glory were of little interest to this son of Ham. Though he had now several sons and daughters, he had no fantasies of founding a nation. While Cush and his followers sought the stars, and established their empire on Earth below, Canaan tilled the soil, trying not to dwell on Noah's hope-filled prediction that his descendants would spawn a "righteous king." It was enough to concern oneself with survival and with the stockpiling of supplies against a bitter winter.

Standing up, he rubbed the small of his back. The stubborn stone had at last come free, but he wished Sherah would call him for supper.

Raising his hand against the late summer sun, he saw that an early snow already robed the northernmost peaks. Sidon had been away upon some journey for months. If he would be coming home for harvest, he had best do so before blasts of frost covered the passes.

The last time Sidon returned, he had brought with him a fair-haired wife. And when he had gone again, the woman, being with child, had stayed on.

Recently, her swollen belly told the world that by autumn's end a new mouth would cry for food in Canaan's house.

No one anticipated that this birth would prevail over all the empires and all the dreams of Ham and Cush. And Canaan did not anticipate what this evening held when Sherah called him from the fields.

As he plodded home, ready to recline before his fire, his wife spurred him. "Come, Husband!" she cried. "No supper tonight! The girl is in labor!"

Very quickly and much too prematurely it happened. By the time dinner would have been cold on the table, the daughter-in-law had placed a wriggling babe in Canaan's arms, asking that he bestow a fitting name.

When the young grandfather peered into the infant's eyes, all thoughts of sweat and hunger dissipated. His heart full of a strange thunder, he whispered, "I think it is best if Noah names this one."

Bundling the babe securely, he raced on foot to the patriarch's village, and finding the elder seated beside his grape arbor, he fell to his knees before him.

"Father Noah," he spoke breathlessly, "see here . . . the son of Sidon . . . is he not a perfect child?"

The old prophet, leaning forward and uncovering the baby's face, was silent a long moment. Then, gaze lifted heavenward, his lips curled in a faint smile.

"He shall be called 'Melchizedek,'" he decreed.

—20—

M elchizedek . . ."
It was, to the folk of Ararat, a most peculiar designation, meaning "righteous king," or "king of righteousness." The people of the mountain whispered it in sarcastic snickers, heads shaking, shoulders shrugging.

There were, at the time, no nations and no kings on Earth. And surely, had there been, no descendant of Canaan could bear a royal scepter!

Perhaps Father Noah was losing touch with reality in his advancing age. Perhaps regret and guilt over the chasm between himself and Ham had pushed him to this desperate length. But if he thought he could win favor in Ham's eyes by naming one of Canaan's grandchildren for nobility, he was sadly mistaken.

The cruelest jokes and the loudest laughter regarding the "king" arose from the Hamitic quarter, down the valley where prosperity reigned.

It would soon escalate to the most blasphemous proportions. For in a few weeks the Hamites would be celebrating their own newborn.

Yes—Cush would be blessed with his own son, and his name would make perfect sense.

• • •

The day little Nimrod was born, the sun blasted over the moun tain like a trumpet.

Nimrod . . . "the strong," his name meant.

He entered life with a shout, rather than with a whimper. The midwife did not need to slap his backside to rouse him, but he came eagerly from the womb, the look of a wrestler on his tiny face.

The moment his parents saw him, they were astonished—even Cush, who was prepared for something great.

The babe had unusual strength, his little arms and legs already muscular, his dark, wet skin reminiscent of the shining feathers of the raven that Noah had first sent forth from the Ark. With amazing intelligence, he seemed to take in his surroundings, the fine home and the luxury of his position, as though he understood at the instant of his arrival just how privileged he was.

Being the model of fleshly strength and confidence, he was destined to fulfill the highest of human expectations.

It was with his advent that Ham and Cush began to look south, toward Shinar, in earnest.

Though their industries were legion on Ararat, and though they had drawn much wealth from the Vale of the Ark, the dream of an empire between the great rivers had never died.

There was no reason to remain at Ararat. The gulf between Canaan and his father was so broad, the affection so strained, that what had once bound Ham to the mountain was no longer an issue.

What *was* an issue, for Ham and for his entire society, was the nearly superhuman glory of Cush's son.

They saw it from his earliest months—the uncanny speed with which he learned to manipulate childish toys, to speak, to think grandly. With the passing years, his physical prowess became legendary.

In stature he was no giant, but at his rite of passage into manhood, when he was only twelve years old, he already stood head and shoulders above many of his fellows. He was, in fact, a genuine spectacle the day he rode through the village of Cush for his debut as a full-fledged adult.

Everyone in the Hamite community turned out for the event— the hour at which his father would present him for acceptance into the tribal council. It was a tradition in this, as well as in the northern communities, that a young man be received into a position of responsibility with some pomp.

But Nimrod, himself, was the pomp of this ceremony. Arriving on the edge of the village common, astride a stamping ebony stallion, his skin gleaming resplendent against a pale yellow robe, he outshone the array of blossoms and tapestries spread along his path. Even the young girls in the crowd, radiant with virginal beauty and with all the comeliness that cosmetics and vivid adornment could supply—even these could not compete with the one who passed before them.

Though musicians had been hired for the event, the rhythm of their march faltered as the young prince rode by. It was hard to concentrate in the presence of such distraction.

Nimrod, who realized the effect he had on the onlookers, was not satisfied to merely ride through town, circle back, and stand before his elders for their blessing. Midway along the course, he drew his steed to a dramatic stance. Then, unclasping his robe, he let it fall to his waist, revealing his perfectly sculpted physique.

Gasps of awe escaped the maidens of the throng. Wives of the elders blushed with admiration, and all the men marveled at the youngster's daring.

Upon his breast was the "insignia of Ham," conceived by the lad himself, and suspended from a gold chain—the stylized form of a raven, not unlike the rebellious bird that had troubled Noah and the family on the Ark.

The obsidian pendant flashed in the sun, just as did Nimrod's fine-chiseled torso. As he struck a perfect pose, allowing his fans to assimilate his glory, he raised a strong hand toward the sky.

"No man elevates me this day!" he cried, his voice resonant with pride. "I was born the mightiest of men! A mighty hunter before the Lord!"

Then passing his arm in an arc before him, as if to take in the farthest stretches of the horizon, he declared, "Let him tremble who dares challenge Nimrod! From this day, the prince is prince no longer, but King of all the Earth!"

— 21 —

The day following his reception, Nimrod rode with his father and grandfather along a high ridge of the Ararat uplands. From the perspective of one jutting pinnacle could be seen the numerous villages that had spread across the valley.

Folks of the various tribes went about their labor on the plain below—some in village streets, most in the fields all around. Flocks of fluffy sheep and herds of red cattle grazed the open areas unrestrained by fences. Herdsmen and shepherds tended them here and there. Women dug in small garden plots outside their tiny houses.

Spring weather promised another fruitful year for the families of Ararat. Field blossoms competed with green grass for the generous doses of sunlight that kept clouds at bay. Industry of the south, unhampered by climate, droned on beneath contented billows of smoke and sulphur.

Nimrod took in the scene with a pounding heart, as Ham and Cush studied him carefully, reveling in the ambition that radiated from his expression.

"Would you have all this be yours?" Ham asked, leaning close to the boy's shoulder.

Nimrod looked into his grandfather's eyes. Without hesitation, he replied, "I believe that it *shall* be mine."

"And so it shall," Ham agreed. "But not without much effort . . . and much blood."

Nimrod cast a furtive glance toward the townships of his great-uncles, and of the patriarch, Noah, whom he had met only a few times in his life. Sighing deeply, he lifted his chin. "They are weak . . . weaker than we . . ."

"Perhaps," Cush assented. "But they have a strength that may surprise you."

"Strength?" the boy laughed. "What strength have shepherds and farmers to compare with the iron and flint of our people? And what

84

gift for the kill? None of them have learned to live off the hunt. It is the hunt which makes the soldier!"

Cush cast a sideways glance at Ham. Always they had marveled at the youngster's militaristic bent. When other children played with dolls and toy wagons, Nimrod had insisted that his father fashion for him small shields and spears. And when other lads had kept close to their mothers' skirts, Nimrod had passed his time in the fields, chasing fleetfooted game, watching the ways of the roebuck, and bringing home more trophies in his first ten years than most men did in a lifetime.

Like an eagle scouting its prey, Nimrod watched the activities of the ant-sized folk at the mountain's foot. As he did, a spark of certainty flashed through his keen eyes.

"Blood is no enemy to me," he affirmed, jutting his strong chin forward. "I shall rise to heaven on other men's blood!"

—22—

A soft summer breeze parted the long fronds of heavy-headed grass in the pasture above Japheth's farm. Melchizedek loved this portion of his great-grandfather's property, as it was secluded by a gentle rise intervening between the grazing field and the village some miles distant.

He followed his sheep as they eagerly pursued a well-worn path to the quiet watering hole in the pasture's shallow basin, and when he had seen that they were all accounted for, he sat down in a billow of soft green tufts.

Laying his staff across his lanky legs and drawing his ankles close to his lithe body, he leaned into a mood of contemplation. How, he wondered, had he been so blessed as to serve as a shepherd in these hills?

To his right, up the mountain, could be heard the bubbling chant of a spring that fed the pond below. A tiny stream descended through a wrinkle of earth between the spring and the clear puddle where the sheep drank. Melchizedek had often mused as to where the water went once it entered the pond, for, except during the rainy seasons, the pool's boundaries never altered.

Great-great-grandfather Noah had once suggested there must be complex underground waterways into which spilloff drained, and likely enormous caverns under the Earth's surface that acted as cisterns to water the land.

Such had been the case in the world before the Flood, when grasses and trees had been supplied with moisture by evening and morning dews, rising from the soil. Now that the sky-canopy had been broken, and rain was a common phenomenon, moisture collected in clouds and was dispensed downward. But surely the planet still contained great pockets of liquid.

Sometimes Melchizedek placed his ear to the ground, listening for the sound of tumbling water and echoing caves. From time to time, he could hear wondrous movements in the Earth, and felt the continual stirring of the new continent.

Melchizedek, much like his great-grandmother Carise, had always been more sensitive to such things than others were.

In fact, there was much about the boy that did not fit a common mold. In appearance, he was a handsome lad with a strong chin and sturdy limbs. In color, he was neither very dark, nor pale. His hair was neither coarse like Ham's nor straight like Shem's. It was lighter than Noah's but not so fair as his own mother's, and he cared little for braids and combs, but wore it free about his shoulders. His eyes were of olive hue, neither blue like Japheth's, nor black like Canaan's. While he bore an agile strength, he was not physically imposing.

Unusually quiet, he had nonetheless won the respect of every farmer and herdsman in the valley by his skills in the wild. He had never practiced much hunting, but he had wrestled more than one bear to the ground and had slain his share of lions when the safety of his sheep required it.

"Life," he maintained, "is a sacred thing."

Canaan had taught him respect for all that had breath, just as *his* father, Ham, had once taught that the good kill is the painless one.

The young shepherd gazed across his little gully to the slopes that cradled the Ark. Often he pondered the riddle of Ham's legacy. *How,* he wondered, *could such disparate tendencies reside within one man?*

It almost seemed that all the misery in this new world derived from this one fellow's unhappiness—an unhappiness that had now spawned the notorious Nimrod.

Melchizedek studied his own slender hands. At the thought of Nimrod, they had clenched into angular fists.

He had never seen his legendary cousin. Were he ever to do so, he knew the meeting would by anything but cordial. All that the "mighty hunter" stood for was alien. How they could be of the same lineage was an inscrutable mystery.

Melchizedek's musings were interrupted by the snap of a twig up the rise behind. Turning around with an eager smile, he was prepared to greet some relative, when he saw it was a stranger who approached.

Suddenly, his breath was shallow, his pulse racing. Though he had never beheld this fellow, he knew him on the instant. Who else would show such a haughty countenance? Who else could match the physique and strength that the legends attributed to his cousin?

"Nimrod?" he said, leaping to his feet and holding his staff like a sentinel.

"The same!" the bold youngster asserted, his voice full of mocking laughter.

"So . . . we meet at last," Melchizedek replied, bowing from the waist.

"Indeed," Nimrod scoffed. "Don't you think it is past time that we met—we, the kings of Earth's two nations?"

Melchizedek lifted his chin. "I am no king, my cousin. Perhaps you consider yourself to be, but I am only a shepherd."

"Ha!" roared Nimrod. "Noah does not think so. Neither does Canaan nor Sidon, nor any mighty man of the north! Why, you were named for royalty from the moment of your birth!"

"That is how you see it," the young man affirmed, "but my uncles, Shem and Japheth, scorn the title. There is no palace and no army in my name. I wear no royal robe, such as yours; I bear no insignia, such as glistens upon your breast."

Nimrod fidgeted with his medallion, giving a perplexed laugh. But suddenly, he snarled, "So, you do not! In fact," he leered, "you look less the part of a king than the servants in my father's house!"

When Melchizedek made no retort, Nimrod's face burned. "Nonetheless," he cried, "you are my enemy!"

The quiet one only shrugged, and turned again to the place where he had been sitting. "I mark no man my enemy," he replied.

The veins of Nimrod's temples throbbed. "Then perhaps you are not just a shepherd! Perhaps you are a brother to the sheep themselves!" he howled. "While I rise to heaven on other men's blood, you shall be scurrying after goats and rams!"

Melchizedek kept his back to the raving challenge. He did not observe that Nimrod lifted his bow from off his shoulder, placed an arrow against the string, and poised it toward the herd at the bottom of the vale.

Swiftly he felled the flock's choicest lamb, and then, with a shriek of hilarity, disappeared over the rise from whence he had descended.

As his hellish laughter rang across the hills, Melchizedek raced toward the slain lamb. Slumping to his knees, he gathered the warm body to his bosom.

Blood streamed from the creature's wounded side, and the lad stared at the heaving ribs until the animal went limp and lifeless in his embrace.

Hot tears sprang to Melchizedek's eyes, and his fists clenched once again. As he glanced up the hill where Nimrod had stood, he knew, for the first time, what it was to hate.

— INTERLUDE —

The old king slumped in his chair, as though the emotion of that long-ago day had never faded.

Little Ali, his companion, hung on each syllable, feeling with his master the depths of his early pain, and longing for revenge.

From the moment Melchizedek had introduced himself into the story, Ali's attention had been riveted more firmly than ever.

"Oh, sir," he marveled, "Nimrod was a wicked fellow! Surely you rose up against him! Surely you did not let him win!"

Clearly recalling how he had felt as a young man, Melchizedek shook his head. "I was a shepherd, not a warrior," he sighed. "But life rarely takes us in the direction we would choose."

"So, you had to fight!" Ali cried, pounding his small fist into this palm.

Melchizedek only nodded.

"Did you have a mighty army?" the boy spurred him. "Were you a great general?"

The old man shrugged, "I will let you be judge of that, once I tell the tale. But, great or not, I was surely the most reluctant soldier ever to raise a sword . . ."

PART III

"And the sons of Noah began to war on each other, to take captive and to slay each other, and to shed the blood of men on the earth, and to eat blood, and to build strong cities, and walls, and towers and individuals began to exalt themselves above the nation and to found the beginnings of kingdoms and to go to war, people against people, and nation against nation, and city against city, and all began to do evil, and to acquire arms, and to teach their sons war, and they began to capture cities, and to sell male and female slaves."

—The Book of Jubilees 11:2
(Lore and Tradition)

War and Rumors of War

—23—

As far as Shem and Japheth were concerned, the destiny that would best fit Melchizedek was the destiny which fit Canaan. Though they revered Noah, they put little stock in the grand title he had given the lad.

Since the boy was content to tend sheep, they were baffled when the antagonism that raged within Nimrod took Melchizedek for its focus. That focus would, ironically, catapult the son of Sidon into the very niche that Noah had defined for him.

The rivalry began in small things—an innuendo passed between Nimrod and his brethren, a comment made in some public address. Before long, the quiet shepherd of Japheth's hamlet was drawing the attention of Ararat society. People already divided along Hamite and anti-Hamite lines were forced to make another political choice: to serve the "King of the World," or to serve the "King of Righteousness."

Bewildered Shemites and Japhethites shook their heads behind closed doors and murmured together in the streets.

Life had once been much simpler: Ham was the "cursed one"; everyone descended from him must, of necessity, be the same.

To side with Melchizedek would be to enthrone a "Canaanite"! But, side with Ham? Never!

Melchizedek watched the growing controversy with equal bewilderment. Never had he striven for anything but the quietness of his hills. He had no desire for fame or contention. He, and all who lived in the north, preferred to avoid the entire matter.

But when Nimrod decided to put teeth to his own ambitions, no one on Ararat, north or south, would have a moment's peace.

• • •

It was a very dark evening over the village of Ham. Carise, who had long been estranged from the fellowship of Ararat, forced years before to set up house in Naeltamauk, shivered as she huddled in the blackness.

Hidden by the shadows outside the village meeting hall, she braced herself against one of the veranda pillars, her heart racing.

With her was her great white tiger, Mandela, whom Canaan had rescued from the sand-bog many years before. She held him close by a glossy tether and cradled her head against his warm flank.

From inside the meeting room, voices of war and intrigue spilled onto the dark summer night. Clasping her fine linen kaftan close to her throat, Carise tried to still the pounding of her pulse, and the fearsome images which the men's conversation suggested.

"How has it gone so far?" she whispered to the cat.

Not only had Ham, Cush, and all their cohorts forgotten the God of Noah, not only had they allowed age-old hatreds to fester on the world's virgin soil, but they were now calling down the blessing of alien deities upon their bloody ambitions.

Carise had witnessed the transition from casual disregard for Yahweh to outright worship of strange gods. At first, she had hoped the symptoms were only superficial, that she imagined them, or that they would pass with time. But in her heart she realized that Cush knew not the One True God, and that those who followed him had no reverence for the Lord.

She had attempted, in Cush's early years, to teach him the paths of goodness, just as she had taught Canaan. But this time, Ham had been too close at hand.

And now, this Nimrod . . .

Her face contorted at the thought of her grandson's treacherous spirit, and she feared this moment, more than ever, that his yearnings for conquest would not long be restrained.

Clinging to her feline companion, she listened as the plot of the would-be warlords floated out on the night air. In prideful tones the dignitaries, whose names would one day be legends, discussed the ease with which they might advance against Noah and his kin.

"Up the Tigris," Eridu was saying, "and across the foothills until we sneak up on Noah's village and Shem's hamlet."

"Meanwhile, Sippar and I will circle in from the west toward Japheth's hamlet," Ur added.

"Just so!" Nimrod agreed. "And when the peasants flee their homes, both sets of them will meet upon the central plain . . . where they will be greeted by my father's soldiers!"

Smug laughter filled the hall as the men congratulated each other on a brilliant strategy. "It cannot fail," Cush affirmed. "Surely the lights of heaven shine on our plans!"

Carise dug her fingers into Mandela's fur, her skin prickling in gooseflesh. The cat turned and licked her face, sensing her anguish.

Her years in Naeltamauk had been more lonely than those in Shinar. Time and again, as she observed the path her menfolk pursued, she wondered if things might have been different had they stayed in the wilderness of the two rivers and never returned to Noah's people.

Was she to blame for the unfolding drama of corruption that typified the southern strain? Perhaps, just perhaps, if she had never forced Ham to contact his father, the two nations could have developed without incident.

Yet she could not have allowed her son, Canaan, to betray all that was natural by marrying his own sister when there were other girls on earth.

"O Mandela!" she groaned, pouring out her sorrow to the sympathetic feline, "I have not seen Canaan in years! Remember, friend, how he saved you from the sand?"

The cat purred, a low, rumbling purr, as though he did remember, and Carise stroked him sadly.

A prisoner of her husband's politics, Carise had never met her own grandson, Sidon, and had never seen Melchizedek.

Suddenly, as the war plot deepened, the woman's sadness turned to anger. Though she had never known Canaan's offspring, she was still their matriarch. Her motherly heart yearned to protect them.

Standing up, she tugged on Mandela's leash and moved out into the night.

She would rouse her personal servants and order a canopied cart loaded for a journey. She must warn her long-lost children of the brewing evil, even if it meant risking her own life.

—24—

Carise knew the general direction in which Japheth's village lay. Nonetheless, she found it necessary to inquire at several places along the way to avoid becoming lost upon the strange road connecting the valley's numerous hamlets.

A curious spectacle she made, traveling in haste through Ararat's foothills, dressed in the finery of a southern aristocrat, escorted by a small retinue of servants, and guarded by a big, white tiger.

When she came upon Japheth's village it was the second morning of her journey. She ordered her chauffeur to lead her cab slowly through the market square, which was full of shoppers and venders. Carefully she surveyed the faces of the crowd, hoping to spy one she might recognize.

She hesitated to ask questions of the people or to let them know who she was. The wife of Ham would not be popular in this region.

She could not help but attract attention, however. All along the way, people stopped to stare at her cab's fringed canopy, at the fine white horses that pulled it, at the well-dressed attendants who accompanied her. And Carise, herself, in bold-striped sari, her headdress of bangles and feathers, captured every eye.

Of course, the tiger, with its glistening, studded collar, was the star of the show. Mandela, whose stride was long, did not appear in a hurry, but could have taken after any threat at a daunting speed. Onlookers kept their distance when the big cat turned his forbidding yellow eyes their way.

At last, though, someone called Carise's name. She jumped nervously. Scanning the throng, she spotted a woman, older than she remembered her, but still a beauty in her own right. "Elsbeth?" she cried. "Is that you?"

The wife of Japheth, who held no small authority in this town, cleared the way for her long-lost sister-in-law. When the cab drew close, she reached forth her ample arms to embrace the flashy woman.

"Yes, it is I!" she replied, climbing onto the seat beside Carise.

Fervently, the two clung to one another, dampening each other with warm tears.

"What brings you here?" Elsbeth cried. "You will be staying with us, won't you?"

"Canaan . . . I must see my son, Canaan," Carise choked. "The news is not good, my sister."

• • •

Canaan's small house was crowded to the walls with Japhethites and Canaanites. Never since he and his bride had taken up residence in the little rock cottage up the trail from Japheth's abode had the simple dwelling been graced by such auspicious guests.

All of the descendants, their wives and husbands, their grown children and grandchildren could not possibly have fit into the parlor, but Sidon and the leading men were present, as well as a number of matriarchs.

Melchizedek had never seen so many of his relations together in one place. The experience might have brought much joy, if the occasion of the gathering had not been so ominous.

Still, though his ears were filled with the dread of war and its rumors, he was awed by more than the tale Carise brought. His great-grandmother was, herself, a wonder, as she sat in the light of the room's small fire, her glorious coppery face full of drama and her hands weaving a spell of urgency with every gesture.

"Friends, you must prepare!" she insisted. "I have related the plot that my menfolk design. They will surely not rest a week before they rush to fulfill it."

"But how are we to trust your word?" someone questioned. "You are, after all, Ham's wife!"

Others murmured agreement, and Elsbeth bristled, ordering quiet. "Carise was always loyal and devoted to Noah when we spent our months upon the Ark!" she recounted. "Despite her husband's treachery, she has always been true to Yahweh!"

"But that was years ago!" someone else laughed. "Things could have changed by now."

At this, Canaan, who sat close to Elsbeth, leaned forward, and pointed a stern finger at the audience. "Some things never change!"

he cried. "Had it not been for the teachings I received at my mother's knee, I would myself be among the southern conspirators. Instead, I have done my best to raise my children in the fear of the Lord."

Carise's gaze lingered over Sidon's countenance as he stood quiet and reflective beside his father. Then she analyzed the face of Melchizedek, who, once again, was struck by the conundrum of his heritage.

Blessings and curses—curses and blessings—what do they all mean? he wondered.

The great-grandmother sensed the riddle that Melchizedek pondered. Looking past the fire, she addressed the group.

"I have borne two sons, Canaan and Cush. One has a heart for God, and one has not. When I held my children in my arms, I knew they could choose their own destinies. Canaan has chosen the way of truth . . . just as I taught him to do."

The village patriarch, Japheth, who had let prejudice blind him for years, shuffled uneasily, but gave no rebuttal.

When Carise, prophetlike, drew a conclusion, Melchizedek felt a tingling in his spirit such as no mountain brook or Ararat breeze could ever have produced.

"From the curse shall arise a blessing," she predicted. "Though fire and blood may usher in his kingdom, there shall arise a righteous priest, one to lay the foundations of a peaceful city, and to herald the coming of the Lord. It falls to us, this day, to choose whom we shall follow."

— 25 —

E vening breezes arising from the southern end of the Ararat Valley brought their own news of war to the folks of the north. For two days after Carise arrived at Adataneses the haunting sound of ritual drums could be heard wafting up from the Hamite quarter.

Though war drums had not been necessary in the advanced society of Adlandia, no one need tell the Japhethites and Shemites that the fearsome reverberations were intended to chill the blood of Ham's enemies.

Doubtless, the patriarch of the southern forces realized by now that his own wife had played the traitor. Her flight for the north would goad him to even hastier action.

There was no telling just how much Carise knew of the planned strategy. But there was no reason to formulate another design. Speediness would ensure Ham's success and, given the primitive state of his enemies' military strength, there was no fear of failure.

As soon as the southern troops could be organized and equipped, they would set upon the northern tribes. The goal would be the elimination of the elder generations and the capture of the young and strong.

Shinar would be built on the sweat of Shemites and Japhethites. And the dream of a Hamite empire spurred the taunting drums to a frenzy.

• • •

According to the conspirators' plot the night Carise had overheard them in the southern longhouse, the Hamite hordes divided into three camps, two of which moved north to close in on the three villages of Shem, Japheth, and Noah.

They did not expect much of a fight, but hoped to funnel the feeble northern defenders down the valley where they would be confronted with armies of Nimrod, Cush, and Ham.

101

In the brief hours between Carise's warning report and the arrival of the enemy, the men of the north did what they could to prepare.

Because they were farmers, not warriors, and because they were not skilled metallurgists, the men of Ararat could do little to arm themselves but sharpen the crude swords and spears that they had received as wedding gifts when they were young, most of which were more ceremonial than functional.

None of the northern villages was fortified. Such security measures had never been necessary. But families hastily constructed barricades at the entrances to their homes and at the town's low gates.

Because Melchizedek had no wife, no children to protect, he was free to offer help wherever it was needed, and spent these tense hours going from house to house, from village gate to marketplace, seeing what needed to be done.

For a quiet young man, this did not come naturally, but necessity fed a leadership ability that had lain dormant in his spirit. Without his hardly seeing it, people drew courage from his calm strength, turning to him instinctively for guidance.

As dark drew on, the second evening after Carise's arrival, the matriarch called for the women and children of the village to meet at the longhouse, and she impressed upon them that they should cloister themselves there.

"Stay put," she told them, "until Melchizedek tells you otherwise. The men of the south will take no mercy on you."

With that, she shut the door to the building and stationed her great white cat as guard.

● ● ●

The morning of the third day, Melchizedek, on a tall, buff stallion, waited with the defenders on the plain outside the town gate. Next to him, on separate mounts, were Canaan and Japheth.

From the western rim beyond the village, rather than from the south as had been expected, the enemy staged their surprising circuitous approach.

With unflinching speed, the cavalry of Sippar and Ur made straight for the untried farmers, war machinery on smooth, round wheels interspersed among them.

Just as the troops and cavalry of Eridu and other southern warlords attacked the Shemites to the east, the well-practiced invaders advanced.

Adlandian wars had been fought from impersonal distances, through the use of missiles and remote-control technology.

This, the first all-out confrontation in the new world, would be hand-to-hand, blood-for-blood, bone-to-bone.

Melchizedek, the young general (for so he was, whether by choice or not), would never forget his first experience of combat. His heart's thrumming in his ears was almost as loud as the oncoming horde, but he had presence of mind enough to know his men must not be stationary prey. He gave a shout and leapt forward, lifting his sword in the air and signaling his troops to do likewise.

Across the western foothills they dashed, swords raised, lashing their meager weapons as though they were not intimidated.

Cries of challenge arose from the Japhethite ranks, the young general's voice lustiest and most daring of all.

As his horse sped forward, its nose splitting the wind, its mane streaming back, the rider felt, for an instant, as though he were watching the drama from a distance, from someplace above it all.

He would remember, later, wondering if this meant he was about to die, if Noah's prophecies concerning his own greatness would be fulfilled entirely on this battlefield.

But just as quickly, he was once again with his body, the feel of the horse's flanks hot against his thighs, the air whistling through his hair.

Suddenly, there was impact. His horse reared backward, tossing its master in an arch. Melchizedek saw the menacing face of one challenger flash beneath his horse's chest, and then he and the other rider tumbled to the ground.

Reflexively, Melchizedek bounded to a defensive stance, his legs spread wide, his sword warning the enemy with a flashing sweep.

When the southerner made a lunge, there was no time for thought, no hesitation. The peace-lover, the man who hated conflict, lunged also, and his sword drew blood before the challenger's could find its mark.

With another quick thrust, the young general brought the enemy to his knees, and in an instant the mortal wound had left him lifeless.

Melchizedek had killed a man.

Before the battle was over, he would take other lives, and before many years would pass, he would take yet more.

But, for now, it was enough to survive, to intervene between death and his own comrades.

—26—

D espite valiant efforts of men like Melchizedek and his hardy followers, the Japhethites were so gravely disadvantaged, so underarmed and so unpracticed, that the battle was not prolonged.

Wave upon wave of invaders soon left them scattered, disoriented. As the afternoon sun shone through clouds of dust, it revealed their defeat.

Those who remained alive were on the run, pushed like a stampeding herd down the Ararat plain. By nightfall, the foothills were strewn with the debris of war.

Melchizedek brought his mount to a stamping halt upon the central plain and checked his bearings. Far away, to his right and to his left, were the glowing pyres of his uncles' ravaged villages. Behind him were hundreds of refugees, a few on horseback, many bundled in overburdened wagons, and most on foot, bearing upon their backs whatever of value they had rescued from their homes.

The southerners had chosen not to annihilate the north, but only to rout them. When the Japhethites fled, the southern forces turned toward the villages, decimating the homes and setting the walls ablaze.

Even then, they spared many, especially the young, the strong, and the beautiful.

The reason was not hard to guess. Of what use could the dead be to Nimrod? Melchizedek knew his people had been spared for a fate worse than death—for slavery and all its horrors.

The young general had lost sight of his grandfather, Canaan, and his other relations who had fought beside him. He hoped they were safe in the throng, which was now doubling in size as hordes of Shemites from Sedeqetelebab joined them.

Where, he wondered, might Noah be? Had he escaped Ahora before it, too, was set in flames?

If so, it would only be to confront the forces of Cush, Ham and Nimrod who would be upon them all too soon.

From south of the plain, they could be seen before they were heard, the torch-lit troops of the south's main army. As the eerie glow of the approaching hordes grew more intense, the fear-wracked refugees huddled together sheeplike, awaiting the raven's swooping kill.

Melchizedek surveyed his followers, thinking how much like his own flocks of lambs and kids they were, and how peculiar that they looked to him for salvation.

How he had come to be at the head of this pathetic congregation, he would never know. But it was apparently up to him to give them guidance.

Pulling an arrow from the sheath upon his bare back, he lifted it skyward. "Listen well!" he cried above the wailing of women and the cries of little children. "We have no escape, but to flee to the mountains!"

At this, the desperate throng peered over their shoulders toward Ararat. But none of them, not even Melchizedek, expected the sight that greeted them.

High on the mountain's moon-lit side, exactly where the Ark was known to rest, dim lights could be seen moving along the old vessel's balustrade.

A shudder of gasps and whispers passed through the crowd, and Melchizedek squinted his eyes to be sure he saw correctly. "Noah . . ." he sighed. Then more loudly, "It is Noah! He has reached the Ark, and bids us flee there for safety!"

Of course! Why had no one else thought of it? Had the ship not saved many lives in the past? Perhaps it could do so again!

Like a stampeding herd, the people turned for the hills, making a hundred paths toward the Ark. Not all of them would reach it before the southern raiders took aim. But the majority would be saved to resist the goals of Shinar.

—27—

T he southern raven was relentless, pursing the fleeing Shemites, Japhethites, and Canaanites to the very heels of Ararat.

Across the dark plain they slaughtered, not discriminating as they had planned, but killing young and old alike, until Nimrod renewed his order to take as many slaves as possible.

As the marauders turned their energies to the taking of captives and the looting of goods left behind on the plain, many northerners managed to reach safety.

When hundreds of the villagers had attained the vessel's sanctuary, Noah snuffed out the lights that had guided their escape, leaving the enemy to blindly scale the heights of the ancient haven. In the black of night it was difficult for the southern captains to make out the Ark's whereabouts.

While the refugees sat within the dark hold, listening for the enemy down the rise, Melchizedek picked his way through the corridors, softly calling his grandfather's name.

At last there was the longed-for response. "Over here, son," Canaan answered. "Everyone is safe!"

Trembling, Melchizedek fell to his knees. In a pale patch of moonlight that filtered through an opening in the Ark's side, he could see his grandfather's outstretched hands. Grasping them fondly, he thanked Yahweh, and then scrutinized those who huddled nearby. Miraculously, all his loved ones, even his estranged elders, Japheth and Shem, had escaped unscathed, and waited together for the outcome.

"Where is Noah?" he asked anxiously.

"Checking on his cargo," Carise replied, a smile in her voice. "How this must remind him of those days upon the Ark!"

"Yes—it does . . ." came a quick affirmation. "Except that this time, many have entered in."

Melchizedek, seeing that Noah had returned, stood to his feet, bowing respectfully. "It has been a long time, Father," he greeted.

Noah studied the lad with wide eyes. "You have done proudly tonight," he said, clapping him on the shoulder. "A true leader of the people!"

"I did very little, sir," he said. "Besides, we lost."

"You took action, while others sat frozen before their predator," Noah countered.

Melchizedek recalled the crowd's sheeplike nature. "I suppose, sir. But what now? What of the hordes who approach?"

Noah had a distant look, as though he thought of a time long past.

"God has shut the door of the Ark to them," he replied. "There is no way that they shall enter in."

• • •

Through the opening in the Ark's siding, left when lumber was needed for Noah's village longhouse, the family watched while the enemy drew near.

Humanly speaking, there was no possibility that if the Hamites breached the walls the people of the Ark would be able to withstand them.

Already the ascending armies had surrounded the vessel, which sat like a nested bird in the mountain's palm. The sound of their victory cries shook the ancient timbers.

But those fearsome shouts were only a prelude to the awesome terror that was about to challenge the mount. Suddenly, from the moon-lit heavens, another cry descended, a sound as from the throne of God on High.

The howling chorus of some great power, and a searing ray of unearthly light flooded the mountainside, shaking the ground and illuminating the troops of Naeltamauk.

Shielding their eyes, the attacking forces fell back, stunned by the brilliance and filled with trepidation.

Grass and pebbles were sucked into a whirlwind, encompassing the Ark, stinging the eyes of Cush's soldiers, and driving Ham's men to the ground.

But, Nimrod, who had no patience with their cowardice, called them to stand tall. Staring full-faced into the flashing storm, he lifted his fist heavenward and cried, "The gods have returned! The gods of Shinar and Olympus! The empire is ours for the taking!"

Then, with a shout, he motioned his men to advance again. But as they did, the tempest howled the louder, until the very foundations of Ararat trembled.

Inside the Ark, weeping and wailing filled the corridors. Melchizedek turned a bewildered face to his kinsmen, but Canaan, the whites of his eyes gleaming wide against his dark skin, had no advice to offer, and the elders, too, were speechless.

Only Noah stood to his feet and drew Melchizedek into a confident embrace. "The time has come, my son!" he said. "This night is your kingdom established!"

The young shepherd's head swam with a thousand questions— but not one came readily to his tongue. He could not know whether it was from his own mind or the mind of Another that he derived his words, but suddenly, he was prompted to speak with an authority and a presence beyond his normal ken.

"Fear not the hounds of hell, nor the Hand of Salvation that drives them back! What Yahweh has preserved shall be forever, and what he has overcome shall never stand!"

Instantly, another searing flash shrieked above Nimrod's armies, and a thunder as of the voice of God overwhelmed the mountain.

It lasted but a moment. In the twinkling of an eye it came and went.

In its wake reigned silence . . . and night black as death.

A sulphurous perfume permeated the atmosphere, and all about the Ark small rocks and debris that had collected in the whirlwind fell in a shower to the ground.

The stunned forces of Nimrod, Cush, and Ham lay still as corpses about the hollow, while Noah's people peered out through the missing siding and over the balustrade, their mouths agape.

One by one the folk of the north passed through the Ark's single door and tiptoed through their oppressors' leveled ranks.

By morning the defeated Hamites would rouse and retreat, wondering at the heavenly war. But there would be dancing in the charred villages of Shem, Japheth, and Noah—dancing and singing before the Lord.

—28—

ollowing the intervention of Yahweh on behalf of the northern tribes, Nimrod knew that to pursue his kingdom he would have to set his teeth in earnest against the Lord. For him, this was a small matter. He and his father already claimed allegiance to strange deities, to the lights of old Adlandia and the eternal Olympian heights.

Besides, he reasoned, Yahweh had been no friend of mankind. Why should he serve a God who had, once upon a time, destroyed Earth and nearly all her inhabitants? If Noah's God wished to sustain the weak and unambitious folk of the mountain realm, let Him do so! The people of the south would bow to gods wiser than Yahweh.

The first evening after the battle, the sound of ritual drums pounded into the smoke-filled air from every Hamite village. Bonfires marked the low gate of each town, and in their flashing glow, dancers pranced and gyrated persistently before the setting sun. Intoxicating drinks and dream-herbs passed from hand to hand about each council circle. Soon, a strand of singing, chanting folk would wend its way from each little city, forming a mighty congregation in the temple square of Ham's capital.

Though Nimrod's armies had not fared well when they attacked the Ark, they still retained the many captives taken on the plain. Several of these would represent each Hamite village, when tonight, Cush invoked the favor of the region's deities upon his son's next venture.

The southern tribes had not been told just what that venture would be, nor had the prisoners been informed as to their role in the coming ceremonies. The fact that they were still bound hand and foot and that they had not been allowed to eat for three days indicated that the honor would not be pleasant.

As the drums beat more ferociously with descending darkness, each chained Shemite, Japhethite, and Canaanite implored heaven to once again intervene.

110

• • •

Ham, Cush, and Nimrod sat on richly embroidered pillows at the head of the Naeltamuk meeting hall. Before them, a limestone slab, the length of a man's body, dripped with the blood of the evening's twenty-ninth victim of decapitation.

Before midnight, fifty northern prisoners would be slain upon this altar.

A dozen elders swayed glassy-eyed before the low pedestal, mesmerized by the "weed of heaven," whose pipes filled the close quarters with an acrid cloud. A monotonous, chanted dirge echoed from the chamber, in cadence with the seductive rhythm of ritual drums, lulling the fold outside to thoughtless acceptance of the cruelty in progress.

Within the brightly lit courtyard, the bound captives waited in line, each dreading the moment when he would be called to step through the temple's curtained door. Once inside, the dark smokiness of the room and the hypnotizing pulse of the unflagging drums would dull the perception of their fate. But they knew well enough, as they waited, that this night their souls would be required of them.

From hand to hand, the council members passed small grey saucers, the tops of their victims' skulls. The shallow containers, which had first been charred over the central fire, had been filled with the blood of the slain. This horrible liquid the elders drank, at Nimrod's direction, for "the strengthening of the heart to war."

Into the night, sparks from the courtyard bonfire lifted the souls of the departed toward the afterlife. No prayers to Yahweh were offered up for them, except those prayers that were their own.

—29—

When morning blasted over the eastern ridge, it exposed the left-overs of an orgiastic scene in the Naeltamauk square. Helter-skelter, the debauched Hamites of a dozen villages lay in drugged and drunken disarray.

Nimrod, fully alert, strode through the passed-out revelers, kicking at the half-clad women who lay among them and shouting to his guards to rouse the people.

"Hold the banners erect!" he commanded, pointing angrily at the toppled standards that the partying sentinels had neglected. Quickly the "Wardens of the Raven," as the color guard was called, dashed for the yellow flags strewn against the gate. Through bleary eyes, they watched their leader as he marched toward the platform at the far end of the square.

As they straightened their disheveled uniforms and let the bird-crested banners unfurl to the wind, they did their best to wake the sodden patriots.

Nimrod was about to make a pronouncement, and he must have an audience.

• • •

"To be as the gods!"

This was Nimrod's motto.

When high noon had burned the fog from the heads of his devotees, he proceeded to lay out for them the "plan of the ages," as he called it.

It would require further warfare, further blood, the taking of yet more slaves, he told them. But it would culminate in an exodus for Shinar, a new trail for humanity blazed by ten thousand feet, down the Tigris corridor!

As the people absorbed the message, a thrill of incredulity and then of mass enthusiasm overtook them. Sweat poured from

112

Nimrod's forehead and his face flushed with glory as the audience raised repeated cheers in the Hamite square. Turning his gaze heavenward, he flung his arms wide, receiving their adulation.

Then, growing somber, he called for silence. Studying his followers as if to determine whether they were worthy of his next revelation, he waited until an awe-filled hush overcame them.

His voice was low and dreadful as he called for the implementation of his greatest dream. "When we reach Shinar," he began, "we shall not only be people of the soil, nor shall we be mighty hunters alone, nor shall our flocks command all our time. We shall not only build great buildings," he informed them, "nor shall we prosper only on merchants' trade. We shall not only be great artisans, and architects, engineers and miners. No, my people," he asserted, his hands working dramatic gestures, "though we shall be and do all these things, and though we shall do them better than they have ever been done, these shall not be the goal of our empire."

Here he took a deep breath, and let the mystery build. "Nor," he continued, "shall we be mighty warriors alone, who subdue the kingdoms of our enemies, until our foes languish beneath our feet! All this we shall accomplish, but it shall not consume all our energy."

An urgent huzzah coursed through the crowd. Heads shook and shoulders shrugged as folks tried to anticipate what could possibly remain.

At last, Nimrod, gleaming as a stormy eagle in his golden garb and flashing pendant, set forth his challenge in strident tones:

"The minions of heaven call us to seek them! The lords of Earth and sky promise glorious things to those whose strength fails not! When we reach Shinar it shall be our purpose to pursue heaven—to grasp hold of celestial truths and make them our own!"

But the people's vision was not as supernal as Nimrod's. Almost he could see it now, rising from the mists of Hiddekel, its pinnacle piercing the clouds, and the wisdom of the immortals passing up and down its spiraled stairway.

"A tower!" he cried, his head thrown back and his veins throbbing with ambition. "A tower to reach heaven!"

His fingers clenched until the perspiration trickled from his crimped palms. The exertion of a thousand workmen was symbolized in his fists as he raised them to pound against the skies.

"We shall build a tower!" he repeated. "And upon its zenith the gods shall be pleased to touch down!"

—30—

Melchizedek sat in a hollow tucked in an isolated corner of
Japheth's Ararat fields—a nook of grazing land even more
hidden than the one he usually frequented. He had been
here for two days, contending that the new mothers of his flock, the
spring ewes, needed a rest.

Actually, he was, himself, in hiding.

The incessant talk of war and fear wearied him. And the propensity of the northern tribes to look to him, an unschooled shepherd,
for leadership, was at times more than he could bear.

Melchizedek made no claim to nor pretense of greatness. Much
more to his liking was the feel of cool grass between his toes, and the
tickle of a lamb's nose against his neck, than the applause or expectation of a million worshippers.

He lay back upon the meadow's bosom and closed his eyes, shut-
ting out persistent images of tramping armies and violent hordes.

But as he allowed the breeze off the Ark's mountain to massage
his soul, a light footstep roused him. Sitting up with a jolt, he
shielded his eyes against the sun, until his great-great-grandfather
made a shadow across his face.

"Noah!" he stammered. "How . . . who told you I was here?"

"What is important is that you *are* here, and not with your people
below," the old gentleman said sternly.

"I could not remain . . . I had to get away," Melchizedek faltered.

"But *they* cannot do so easily," the patriarch pointed out. "There
are more rumors from Naeltamauk, my son. Nimrod threatens again
to strike."

The young man looked across the meadow, a scowl darkening
his brow. "What am I to do about it?" he objected. "I have no training
. . . no experience for leadership."

"You have your credentials," the elder said, sitting down beside him.

"My royal title!" the shepherd laughed. "Father, on this matter we
are not agreed. A king, after all, should have a choice in calling,

should he not? I was never given any choice!"

At this, Noah leaned back, laughing heartily. "Kings may be kings by right of conquest, but most are born to it, with no choice whatsoever. As for you, you were born to it by God above!"

When Melchizedek shook his head sadly, his eyes misting, Noah spoke more gently. "Your people need you, son. The coming years will be hard ones. You must teach them the things of war—you whose feet have longed for peaceful paths."

"But, why me, Father?" the lad countered. "I have done nothing to deserve the calling. Furthermore, I am confused by a good many things."

"Such as?" Noah asked.

"This man, Nimrod. He is a bloody and wicked fellow. Yet he seems to have a heart for things above. Is it improper, Father, to desire heaven? To seek to reach the stars or to long to walk with greater knowledge?"

"You speak of the tower, which he dreams of building."

"Yes . . ."

Noah sighed and drew very close, almost speaking in a whisper, for the topic they approached was holy. "There are only two ways to seek truth, my boy," he said, "and two paths one can take to seek heaven, no matter how many names they may go by. Nimrod will strive, according to the flesh, to be as the gods, to have their knowledge and to raise up legions in his own name. But the man who finds God Almighty desires no greatness for himself, nor does he climb the ladder of holiness on rungs made by human hands. He strives, like Enoch of old, to live a pure life and to please the Lord with his heart."

"Enoch . . ." Melchizedek mused. "I have heard of him. The prophet of antiquity, before the Flood." He thought back to the tales passed among the Japhethites regarding this ancient sage. "No one knows what became of him, do they, Father?"

Noah shook his head. "Enoch simply walked with God, and then he was no more, for God took him," he replied.

Melchizedek trembled, his skinned covered with goosebumps. "He must have been a very holy man," he sighed.

"And yet," Noah assured him, "he was nothing *more* than a man."

The old counselor's tone troubled Melchizedek greatly, for it indicated that the youngster's own destiny might be as mysterious as Enoch's.

Suddenly, the shepherd stood to his feet, grasping his staff and trying to shake the eeriness the words produced.

Imagining the grip of cold iron within his fists, he turned the staff round and round. "Perhaps weapons and warfare would suit me after all," he assented. "At least for a little while. . . ."

Noah stood with him and placed an arm about his shoulders. "Yes . . . for the moment. And for however long it takes. God will be your armor and your shield."

— Interlude —

It was the very darkest hour of the night, but Ali could not have slept on the softest pillow.

Fantastic images raced through his young mind as he envisioned the horrors of Nimrod's ambition and the excesses it spawned.

"I do not understand, Master!" he exclaimed. "Even after Yahweh forced Nimrod's army to retreat, he still fought against the truth."

Melchizedek nodded. "Pride, my boy," he affirmed. "It was pride that drove my cousin. He could not sit still as long as there was something or someone higher than himself."

To Ali, the notion of The One True God was foreign. But he was coming to believe, through his master's witness, that there must be such a deity.

"So, did he build his tower?" Ali asked, his eyes wide with wonder. "A tower high as heaven?"

"It was his unrelenting goal to do so," the king replied. "But God had plans, as well . . ."

PART IV

"*And they said, Go to, let us build us a city and a tower, whose top may reach unto heaven . . .*"

—Genesis 11:4a

"*And Noah wrote down all things in a book . . . . And he gave all that he had written to Shem, his eldest son. . . . And Noah slept with his fathers and was buried on Mt. Lubar in the land of Ararat.*"

—The Book of Jubilees 10:13–15
(Lore and Tradition)

The Tower

—31—

For fifty years warfare was a way of life on Ararat. During that half century, the face of the land so altered that one coming upon it from a long absence would not have recognized it.

Save for the looming mountain and the familiar foothills, the range of ridges and mighty highlands that formed the backdrop, nothing was the same.

The small villages and tiny hamlets that had once dotted the valley were no more. In their place had arisen cities with walls and turrets, fortified gates, and guard towers. Not only were the tribes of the north mortal enemies of the south, but among themselves, even, they were not always amiable. From time to time Shemites and Japhethites turned on one another, and the Canaanites, while being the line from which the northern king had arisen, still struggled for respect.

As for Melchizedek, the reluctant ruler, he bore within his peaceful breast the heart of a military leader. When not overseeing the management of the restive northerners, he was often challenged by Nimrod's dream of conquest. A dozen times in these fifty years, he was forced to go warring against his cousin.

Though Yahweh never again intercepted a southern attack as dra matically as the night the Ark was threatened, he did bless Melchizedek. Nimrod learned not to underestimate the shepherd-king's military savvy, and when the southern hordes were quiet, prosperity graced the mountain.

To the benefit of both regions, trade relations managed to survive most of the feuding. The highland tribes had developed their own industries, modest in comparison to those of Cush, but sufficient for their more modest ambitions.

Once he had taken up the royal call in earnest, Melchizedek established his own headquarters—a magnificent palace, central to the three tribes. Though the people of the mountain were not as wealthy as the Hamites, they spared no expense in outfitting the king's house. And it rivaled, grace for grace, the glory of Nimrod's domicile.

Tonight Melchizedek sat alone upon the rooftop of his private suite, a cluster of small, simply decorated chambers on the north side of his castle. From this vantage point, he could take in the slope that held the Ark and survey the sky above it.

He had sent all his servants away, wishing to have solitude. And he passed the evening as he often did, in silent communion with the God who had trodden shepherd trails beside him.

He fingered the gold fringe upon his robe and stared blankly at the wrought silver chalice that held his wine. He envied those who lived in meadow huts and drank from clay cups. He would prefer to find Yahweh in a field flower than try to remember him amid the glamour of royal trappings.

Though he had donned the habit of monarchy to please his subjects and to fulfill the station appointed him, he had never ruled with a scepter. His shepherd staff had always been his royal baton. He was never without it, and even now he eyed it fondly where it leaned against the rooftop balustrade.

Lifting it gently, he stroked the gnarled wood which his grandfather, Canaan, had carved for him years before. Then he held it aloft, playfully arcing the crook over the full moon's outline, as if to capture the silvery orb for himself.

As he did this, his mind was transported beyond the blue sheen of moonlight. Suddenly, it seemed he was surrounded by a warm hush, tangible as a mother's caress, but inviting him to be strong and fearless.

The king's heart stood still as he recognized the Lord's presence. It had been half a century since he experienced such a thing. Not since the night Yahweh had spoken through him on the Ark had Melchizedek known such urgency and such power.

Drawing his robes close, he stood to his feet. "Speak, Lord," he whispered. "Your servant hears."

"The time of division is at hand," the Voice began. "The roots of Ararat reach forth across the Earth. Fear not the arm of flesh, whose cities rise, only to die. But take up your destiny, the order of your priesthood, and seek the land to which I lead you. For its foundations are forever."

—32—

That same night, as Melchizedek listened to the Lord's peculiar directive, another king heeded different promptings, in the distant capital of Ham's realm.

Seated upon the balcony of his richly adorned bedroom, Nimrod watched as his court magicians labored over the reading of herb leaves in a shallow saucer at his feet. For two hours they had debated as to whether or not this was an opportune time for war, and whether or not the exodus for Shinar should be attempted soon.

The energies of the southland during these five decades had focused on the development of large religious centers, temple compounds, and gigantic structures that were a preliminary to the tower of Nimrod's dreams.

Though he intended one day to abandon the Ararat valley, to take his people and his slaves to the golden land of Hiddekel, he was eager to invoke the blessings of the gods even in this locale.

Surely if they saw his devotion, the lengths and expense to which he went to honor them in this place, they would in turn honor his hopes for the future. Perhaps they would even show themselves once again, to lead his nation forth into the new country.

This moment, as he waited impatiently for his sorcerers' conclusion, he longed more than ever for some direct word from the deities he revered.

"Get on with it, you worthless ones!" he snarled, leaning forward and shaking the seers by the shoulders.

"We approach an agreement, Your Majesty," the eldest said, bowing before the offended king.

"Then, if only one or two of you dissent, let the majority rule!"

The wizards consulted together once more, and finally, with a relieved sigh, the elder again reported.

"The discrepancy, sir, lies not over whether the time is ripe for the exodus to Shinar, but over whether it will follow on the heels of another war. We advise that you be ready to depart, though the fight may not be necessary."

Nimrod sat back in his chair, with a bewildered shake of the head.

"Are you suggesting I might sneak out of the valley like a slinking dog? Fools!" he cried. "I shall go out with a blast of trumpets, and with a thousand more slaves in tow than I have won thus far!"

The magicians glanced at one another, then studied the floor in silence.

"Now be gone!" Nimrod demanded, his face flushed with anger. "And when you go, call Ur and Eridu to the council hall. Summon my father and grandfather with them! The day of our glory arises, and the gods await its dawning!"

• • •

In full regalia, banners waving, shields gleaming, the armies of Nimrod headed up the valley toward the cities of Noah. They came in one vast wave, spread shoulder to shoulder across the plain. Their drums declared their approach and their intention to trample anything in their way, to loot and capture all of value and any person of strength or youth.

In this one final move, they planned to destroy all that the northern allies had worked for in the past half-century, to bid them adieu in a bloodbath, and to depart for the new country, conquerors of the Earth.

They expected retaliation. Spies between both nations were so clever that no military venture could be undertaken without the enemy being informed. What they did *not* expect was to find mile after mile of silence, of undefended territory, with no sign of soldiers, trenches, horses, or weapons.

When they had ridden far past the rim of the northern nation and had not yet found a single impediment to their entrance, they grew uneasy.

The burgs along the wilderness, unprotected by tall walls and turrets, were quiet, their residents having sought sanctuary in the large cities further up the plain. This was no surprise. Entering one after another, the troops took whatever valuables they could carry in their girdles and pouches and continued to tramp.

What *was* a surprise was that when the great towns came upon the horizon, their gates were open—no guards stood watch along their walls, and no trumpets blared to warn the inhabitants.

Instead, as Nimrod sat astride his stallion, Ham on one side of him and Cush on the other, and as they waited at the head of their silent army, five dim figures advanced across the plain.

Joining one another in front of the invading horde, they were easy to identify.

Noah and Shem had ridden out from the east, Japheth and Canaan from the west, and Melchizedek had left his palace to meet them on the central plateau.

The radiant young king was spectacular. Dressed in purest linen, riding a horse so white its mane flashed in the winter sun, he, with his shepherd's staff borne proudly beside him, symbolized righteousness.

For a long moment the five allies stood motionless before their enemies. The three southern captains stirred restlessly in their saddles. Ham was especially moved by the sight of his firstborn, Canaan, who bore neither shield nor bow and who observed his father with sad eyes.

But Nimrod, ever the rebel, set his jaw proudly and hailed them all. "We come not as friends!" he cried. "We come to make war! Men of the north, where are your armies?"

Again, the five confederates were silent. At last, Noah moved out from the alliance, his gaze piercing the young warlord to the soul.

"There shall be no battle today," he announced.

Nimrod gawked at him incredulously. When the old patriarch stood his ground, saying not another word, the challenger gave a nervous chuckle.

"I have declared war!" he reiterated. "Who shall stand against Nimrod?"

Once more, the allies were unmoving as Noah let silence settle over the haughty prince like a damp mantle. At last, approaching Ham, the patriarch confronted him with authority.

"Years ago, you chose a path of rebellion," the old father began. "I welcomed you back to Ararat, as the child of my bosom. I gave you one of the daughters of Japheth for Canaan's wife, and your firstborn has been an exemplary citizen."

Ham looked at the ground, shame clouding his features.

"I told you then that if you ever chose to leave, you would not take Canaan with you," he reiterated. Then, in a loud voice, he proclaimed,

"Neither shall you take another thing which pertains to this mountain, for it is the possession of Melchizedek, seed of Canaan's line!"

Nimrod's horse gave a jittery snort as the rider shifted angrily. But Cush restrained the animal and gestured to Nimrod to keep silence.

"You know, then, our intention to leave for Shinar?" Ham acknowledged.

"Such a thing could not be kept secret," Noah replied.

"You have no power to stop this army!" Ham objected. "You only make our way easy to enter your cities and take what we will!"

Noah nodded. "So it would seem. This you have done, over and over, though we have fought you valiantly. But, it shall not happen again," he warned. "By the spirit of God Almighty, I tell you, as you leave for Shinar, you shall take not another thing which belongs to this mountain. Neither gold nor silver, animals, men or women. The Lord has laid out the dividing rod. There shall be no war today!"

Nimrod was impatient. He would have slain the old man on the spot. But Cush, closer to Ham's generation, tingled with fear as the prophet spoke. As for Ham, his soul shook. Though he had long ago turned to his own way, he knew his father was a holy man, and that what he spoke always came to pass.

This time, when Nimrod bolted, raising his sword in a flourish, it was Ham who intervened. "Enough!" he cried. "Put your weapon in its sheath!"

Dumbfounded, the proud prince let the sword go limp, lightning flashing through his eyes.

Ham feigned nonchalance. "What need have we for what belongs to Canaan?" he spat. "Let the mountain people keep their sheep and goats! We have greater things to pursue."

Turning his own horse about, the dark patriarch sped back through the ranks of his armies, toward Naeltamauk. Nimrod, seeing that Cush would do likewise, at last gave order to retreat.

As the mighty prince followed his troops down the plain, he never once looked back at his cousin. Chagrin marked his countenance, and he preferred that Melchizedek not see it.

— 33 —

Melchizedek reined his horse over the rise leading down to Canaan's cottage. A wild wind blew off of Ararat tonight, bringing with it sleet and driving snow. The king's buff steed pressed against it as the rider spurred him over the hill and urged him on toward the warm lights of the distant dwelling.

The family did not expect him this evening. He had sent no word ahead. In fact, he had come without attendants and had left no message at the palace as to his destination.

Years before, he had begged Grandfather Canaan and Grandmother Sherah to come live with him in the palace, but they had preferred to stay in the simple abode that they had occupied since their youth.

To his delight, his own mother had taken up residence with him during Sidon's extended absences. But Great-Grandmother Carise, who had never returned to Naeltamauk, dwelt with Canaan, savoring each day with the son who had been denied her so many years.

As his horse stopped before the house's low door, the king felt the tension of his high office dissipate. An evening beside Canaan's fire was more to be desired than ten thousand banquets. And an hour of Carise's stories was worth a hundred singing jesters.

More than the anticipation of pleasure made him eager to be here tonight, however. He planned to speak with his grandfather of the strange words the Lord had given him the week before the encounter with the southern captains.

He had shared with no one the peculiar prompting to "seek the land" that God would show him. He could not imagine the meaning of the directive and had feared to speculate upon it. The time had come to gain the counsel of his grandfather, the one who had raised him to please Yahweh in all things.

Dismounting, he went to the window and peeked into the house, allowing himself a private moment to enjoy the scene inside.

As usual, it was the idyllic picture he always carried in his mind concerning home.

Sherah and Carise sat before the fire, doing needlework and chatting amiably. The big white tiger, Mandela, long-lived like his human companions, lay stretched out in lazy luxury beside the hearth. And Canaan whittled in the corner, making some toy for the village children.

At last, going to the door, Melchizedek lifted the latch, calling softly into the warm room.

Sherah dropped the needlework in her lap, and the great-grandmother held out her arms, bidding Melchizedek to join them.

"Your grandfather was just saying how he longed for a visit from you!" Sherah exclaimed.

"Yes, I was!" Canaan said with a smile, beckoning him to get comfortable.

Sherah scurried to fetch a bowl from the sideboard and ladled a heaping portion of lentil soup from the pot suspended above the fire. As Melchizedek enjoyed the simple fare, bending down now and then to stroke Mandela, he found the meal much more to his liking than the delicacies of the palace.

Canaan observed perceptively.

Though the next two hours were spent in familial conversation and light-hearted laughter, when the women retired for the night, the grandfather turned matters to a more serious vein.

"You will be staying until morning?" he asked.

"Of course," Melchizedek replied.

"Good. I suspect you have something on your mind which will require time to discuss."

Melchizedek glanced at the elder in surprise. Remembering that Canaan had always understood him well, he laughed. "Yes, that is true. I should have expected you would see it."

Then, growing somber, the young king reflected. "Do you recall the words which Noah spoke the day we met Nimrod upon the plain? How the Lord had 'laid out the dividing rod'?"

"I do," Canaan remembered. "I wondered what he meant."

"Well," Melchizedek explained, "I fear he meant more than the exodus to the south, and the elimination of the Hamites from Ararat Valley."

Canaan pondered this, his dark eyes brooding. "Do you think you have the interpretation?" he asked.

"It seems so, though I do not understand the end from the beginning."

As he relayed the words which Yahweh had given him, and which echoed the sentiment of Noah, Canaan was amazed.

"'The time of division'?" he marveled. "You are to leave this mountain just as Nimrod left it?"

"For some reason that I do not comprehend, this is what the Lord has shown me," Melchizedek affirmed.

"Buy why . . . where?" the elder wondered.

"I was hoping you could help me with that question," the king said.

For a long while Canaan said nothing, overwhelmed as much with the thought of his grandson's going as with the test to which he was put.

At last, he shrugged. "This is a matter too high for me," he whispered. Then, leaning forward, he grasped the king's knee. "It is a matter for prayer. We shall seek a sign, and we shall expect it on the morrow."

• • •

Long into the night, the two men practiced the art of prayer, which Canaan had perfected during years of labor in the fields.

No vain repetition marked their approach to the Almighty, no silly circumlocution. Straight to the point they came, and by bearing one another up through the weariest hours of darkness, they made their prayers effective.

At early dawn, when the embers of the family fire were nearly dead and his grandfather sat slumbering in his chair, Melchizedek watched him with an aching heart. How he would miss this man who had been closer to him than his own father!

He would always remember childhood years spent at Canaan's side as he taught him how to work a hoe and tend a nursing ewe. To the elder, who did not segregate farming from shepherding but found it necessary to perform both professions, all work of the earth was honorable. And for Melchizedek, the lessons of field and pasture were applicable even to the work of the throne.

The single sorrow of *the king's* life had been the mystery of his father Sidon's peculiar lifestyle, and he often wondered why the man was so rarely home.

Melchizedek had been blessed with the guidance of godly fellows. Noah and Canaan had loved him more than twenty men who knew not Yahweh. But why had he been denied the intimacy that a son should have with his own father?

As he watched Canaan's chest rise and fall in sleep, he reached forward to cover him with the light blanket kept near the chair. Then, prodding the ashes of the fire, he rose to fetch wood from the pile outside the door.

Morning was just creeping over the eastern hills, lighting up the distant mists of the westland, when he gathered a bundle of kindling and turned back for the house.

As he did so, his eyes were caught by the sight of a familiar figure traveling toward Ararat from the westerly realm of departing night.

"Father!" he whispered breathlessly.

Indeed, it was Sidon, returning once again from some quest for adventure. By the expression on his face and the bounce in his step as he hailed Melchizedek, it seemed this trip had been unusually gratifying.

"Son!" he cried, coming upon him with a fervent embrace. "I am so glad to find you here. I have the most wondrous news!"

The king hugged him warmly, still marveling that he should appear today, when his thoughts had been so full of him.

"Always you have wondrous news, Father!" Melchizedek teased. "Some glorious new valley or mountain which I should go to see."

"No, no, my son," the man asserted. "This is no mere valley or mountain. I have at last found the sea! The great waters that once bordered the world!"

"Truly?" Melchizedek exclaimed. "That *is* a find!"

"And one which you *must* witness!" Sidon insisted.

Then, full of conviction, he swore, "But this is not the half of it! The land that flanks the sea is surely the most luscious on Earth! A land flowing with milk and honey . . . A land fit for a Canaanite!"

—34—

D ust, lifted by ten thousand travel-hardened feet, rose into
the sun-drenched air of the Tigris corridor. For weeks the
people of Nimrod had been on the trail to Shinar, a trail
blazed by Ham and previously ventured only when he and his small
family had come and gone upon it.

The prodigal patriarch, second son of Noah, was returning this
time without his wife and without Canaan, the son to whom he had
first entrusted Shinar's mysteries. He led the congregation with a
somber face, having said little since leaving Ararat.

Despite his life of rebellion, he had always retained the sense that
he could, at any time, retrace his path, return to his father and to the
God of his childhood. Today, as he pursued the final leg of his trek
toward a lifelong dream, thousands of people having embraced his
ambition, he was less than perfectly content.

He knew that this time, there was no turning back. Though he
had never considered it important to have Yahweh's blessing, the fact
that he had now spurned the Lord entirely was a fearsome thing.

He tried not to dwell on the realization. He tried to think on the
glories that lay ahead.

But those glories were, now, somehow hollow.

Cush may not have felt the emptiness. Nimrod surely did not. As
Ham observed the self-proclaimed King of the World, he knew that,
indeed, he saw only a golden road ahead.

Nimrod bore himself regally as he rode alongside his grandfather.
Behind him a file of beautiful women trailed, wives for his bed-
chamber and concubines for his pleasure, reclining in canopied cabs
which were borne upon the shoulders of Shemite slaves or towed by
handsome horses.

Following them marched file upon file of uniformed troops, the
hardy warriors who had captured for Nimrod a nation and a name.

And beyond stretched countless hopefuls, citizens of his empire-
to-be, their possessions stacked in wheeled wagons or upon the backs

of Japhethite captives, whose sweat would build the country.

As Ham considered this latter element of the exodus, the folk who came not willingly, but at spearpoint and in chains, a chill crossed his shoulders. Their spirit had not been broken. Shemites still evinced hearts of cold iron, and Japhethites and Canaanites showed a patience borne of hope for revenge.

But ahead, through the purple mist of evening, lay the land that had thrilled Hamite imaginations for years. As the great company filtered toward it, as they glimpsed it for the first time, a rush of amazement and then a mighty cheer arose from their ranks.

Shields clattered and spears caught the dusk along their points, glinting violet against the sunset haze.

Ham's energy rose with the hope of his people, allowing his fear of the future to settle temporarily with the dust.

—35—

For many northerners, the exodus of the southern nation
left a hopeless void. Among those who had departed were
captive sons and daughters, brothers, sisters, wives, and
children of the north.

Some of these had been enslaved for years to the Hamites, having
been taken in the earliest battles against Melchizedek. Others were
victims of more recent invasions. But so long as they had been in
bondage to a people who resided nearby, there was hope that they
might one day be reclaimed. Now that they had been ushered out of
the Valley of the Ark, faith that they could ever rejoin their families
was hard to maintain.

Had it not been for this heartbreak, the northerners might have
more easily accepted a new ordinance of God, which was proclaimed
this day before the nation. As it was, the news that Melchizedek must
leave the mountain came as an inscrutable blow.

From the platform on which the Ark rested, Noah explained that
the king had been called to dwell in a distant and uncharted land. The
people, ranging far down the hillside, listened sadly, wondering why
this must be. But whys and wherefores were not addressed because
there had been no unveiling of God's purpose.

Melchizedek, who knelt before the prophet, kept his head
bowed as Noah reminded the murmuring populace that his
kingdom was not so much territorial as spiritual. "Think not," he
warned them, "that his calling is confined by boundaries, or that
the God he represents reigns over a single region. Yahweh is Lord
of the whole world, and the priest of his domain is priest of the
Earth!"

With these words, Melchizedek recalled the tale of Enoch. A chill
crept up his back, and he drew his royal mantle close.

But the aged patriarch lifted him to his feet so that he stood
facing the other elders who flanked Noah on each side. Shem,
Japheth, and Canaan watched in wonder as Noah placed in the king's

133

hands a peculiar offering, a silver tray strewn with broken bread and a goblet of wine from the Ahora vineyard.

"Serve this to your brethren," he directed.

Melchizedek contemplated the mysterious fare, and then reverently passed the gift among the triad of leaders.

Canaan's eyes misted as his grandson performed this service. Japheth obediently received his portion. But when Melchizedek offered the little meal to Shem, that elder took it in trembling hands.

For one unforgettable moment, the King of Righteousness and the eldest son of the prophet fixed their gazes upon one another.

Something of a unity was born through that exchange. Though both men sensed it, it could not be phrased in words. Rising above the prejudices that had long separated them, it was a transcendent thing, like the kingdom of which Noah had spoken.

As Melchizedek turned to pass through the throng, making his way down the mountain toward his father Sidon's waiting caravan, hundreds departed for the unknown land along with him.

But most stayed behind and wept.

It was not for every man to venture forth from Ararat. The majority must remain, and in future years there would be other lands and even more distant realms to populate.

Of all those present, Canaan felt the loss of Melchizedek most personally. Watching his grandson join Sidon on the plain, and tracing their slow exit to the west, he slumped to his knees.

Reaching down, Noah placed a consoling hand on Canaan's head.

"The Lord is with them, my son," he whispered, "as He has always been with you."

—36—

W hen Melchizedek followed Sidon's lead out from Ararat, he had little idea of the length of time it would take to reach the land of his calling.

Though there were no alien countries lying en route, Sidon had described to him some of the more arduous aspects of the journey: the waterless deserts, the icy mountain passes, the treacherous river crossings.

But Sidon, being a free spirit, had never traveled with a great company of people, and so could not have calculated the needs of women and children, or the logistics of such an exodus.

All together, the eight-hundred-mile journey would take a full half year to accomplish.

Taking a direct westerly route out from the Ark's mountain, they followed the meandering streams that became the mighty northwest crook of the Euphrates. The canyons through which it flowed were cold in the shade, hot in the sun.

It was summer, so ice and snow were battled only in the highest ranges east of the Anatolian Plateau, which formed the heart of what would one day be western Turkey.

But wild beasts, precipitous inclines, and bone weariness were continual challenges.

The post-Flood peoples knew that the world had been incredibly altered by the deluge, but they could not realize the full extent of that alteration.

The most cataclysmic change had been the break-up of the planet's single continent, and the resultant division of Earth's waters by seven major land masses.

There had been no part of Adlandia that could not be reached on foot. Noah's descendants would discover, in time, that there were enormous stretches of water bridged by no land at all, and that some of the separate smaller continents, taking the place of the original, could be linked only by water travel.

For now, however, the hopes of these pilgrims lay not in the creation of a world-wide community, but in the the founding of one new city, a city free of war and the animosities that had darkened life on Ararat.

It was true that there was no war, presently, on the mountain. Life had stabilized, and there was no driving political reason to draw apart from the fellowship of kindred people.

What compelled these pilgrims was a nameless thing, something that called to the depths of the human spirit, and which had its roots in a primeval unity even more ancient than Adlandian society.

The oldest legends said that before the Overlords corrupted humanity, there had been a perfect world, a world centered on knowledge of the Divine and revolving around daily communion with the Creator.

The legends called the world Eden, Paradise, Elysium, or Nirvana, a garden of sinless beauty. Also, the legends placed that garden at "the center of the earth," a vague designation, if not geographic, at least spiritual, indicating that all creation had begun there and moved out from there.

Of course, the legends went on to say that Eden had been invaded by evil, and that God, after driving the evil out, had shut the garden off from human habitation.

After that, in the pre-Flood world, there had been something missing, something yearned for that drew the human heart toward the center of the continent.

Pagan legends grew up that the home of the gods was that shut-off place, unattainable by mankind, but always longed after. The mists of Eden became the heights of Olympus, the heart of Adlandia.

That yearning for "center," for "centeredness," had been carried down, through the deluge, to the founding of the new world. But it seemed even less attainable now that people did not know where the earth began and ended, what the borders and boundaries were.

They still felt that the "holy land" lay somewhere. But they did not know where.

Perhaps it was this longing for that center that would ultimately draw people to the fabled land toward which Melchizedek traveled.

Unbeknownst to humanity was the fact that the garden-strewn land that had captivated Sidon's interest and the interest of all who had seen it was as true to "the center of the earth" as could be had on the post-Flood planet.

Were the separate continents of Earth to be fit together, puzzle-like, the general center would be the land to which Melchizedek now journeyed.

It was a mystical place, and its mystique would only become more apparent as people put down roots there.

Today, however, the journey westward was focused not on supernal things, but on survival—the hour-to-hour battle with elements, steeps, food rationing, exhaustion.

To fend off wild beasts, the pilgrims camped in a large circle, the younger and weaker sleeping in the center, and fires were kept burning all along the perimeter.

The travelers had needed to cross several swollen streams along the way, and they had learned to manage the hazardous task quite well. Using inflated rafts made of animal skins, they lashed their belongings to the sides and rode out the white waters with minor incident.

The watery border that stood between them and the golden land one day to be called Syria was their last serious challenge. This was the westernmost bend of the Euphrates. Once they crossed, they could follow it south toward a glorious mountain, one day to be called Hermon, at whose feet, years hence, the gem-like city of Damascus would spread out.

The eternally snowy heights of Hermon beckoned them from many miles away. They hoped to be there within three days.

But first, the river must be forded.

"I have gotten to the mountain in a day by floating the river," Sidon told Melchizedek. "But such a feat would be impossible for a company this size. We must cross over, and then proceed on foot."

Spring runoff from the Anatolian heights still swelled the river to its crest. There was no whitewater where they would ford, but the challenge was just as dangerous, for the smoother rapids concealed depths that surged downstream at a deadly rate.

Following the now-familiar routine, the people began to inflate their rafts, a task which, in itself, took two hours.

Then, after the hardiest swimmers had managed to go over, stringing guide ropes across the water, families, one-by-one, rode their rafts, clinging to the ropes held taut by strong men on each shore.

Evening was drawing on when one of the last families, a young man, his pregnant wife, and a toddling boy set out to cross.

The woman rode in the center of the well-made raft, gripping handles made of leather straps. Her small son sat behind her, hugging her about her distended middle.

The husband, who had managed the feat before with no problem, launched out behind them, pushing the raft ahead of him and kicking his strong legs with powerful thrusts.

Suddenly, something snapped, a lash that circled the raft, and from which were suspended their few belongings. The lash sprang back, slapping the husband in the face and temporarily stunning him.

He managed to hold on to the raft, but it had been thrown off balance, catapulting the wife and child into the frigid river.

Although quick-thinking men jumped in to save them, they were barely able to rescue the young father without being swept under themselves.

Cries of horror and grief arose from the onlookers on both shores, and the few remaining on the east bank wondered what this meant for them.

The swimmers pulled the valiant young man onto the west shore, where he watched aghast as his family was swept away.

Melchizedek, who stood with the final few, not ready to cross until all his flock had gone through, sank to his knees on the muddy incline.

Why now, after they had crossed five hundred miles of treacherous country, should this happen?

The king was numb, having not even the strength to ask the question.

— INTERLUDE —

The old king sat back in his chair, his chin on his chest, as though he were exhausted. His face was very sad, as if the story he had just told had happened only yesterday and not generations ago.

Ali could see that reliving that hard event had resurrected it all too clearly, and that the kindly old gentleman had taken it as a personal failure that he had lost that small family of followers to the deceptive river.

The boy did not speak, respecting Melchizedek's private ruminations. When, at last, the storyteller acknowledged his listener's sympathetic silence, he said, "You see, I was not always a king. As I told you, I began as a shepherd. The desire to keep my flock safe never left me. A shame it is to a shepherd to lose any of his flock . . ."

The perceptive lad exclaimed, "But, sir, your strength lies in the fact that you did not give up. You came on to this country, and you did build your city!"

Melchizedek nodded. "You are a good friend, my boy," he said, reaching forward and patting Ali on the knee. "I suppose you are right. What is important is that I and my people proceeded to do the will of God. We built our city, and it is a grand place, don't you think?"

With this, he stood up from his chair stiffly, and walked to his balcony. Ali, sensing that he should follow, went with him and looked over the rooftops of Salem, spread out white in the moonlight.

Up the rise from the palace the glorious rock-crowned Mt. Moriah, whose name meant "Wisdom Teacher," glistened under the night sky.

And just beyond the rock, a modest temple graced the hilltop, its slender, pearly columns fronting the holiest chamber in the land of Canaan.

It was there that Melchizedek would, tomorrow, offer up the annual atoning sacrifice slated by the priestly calendar.

"The people of our exodus continued down from the north," he said, pointing in the direction of Jericho, and further, Damascus, cities which had not even existed at the time of his journey.

"We followed the Jordan River, along the divide that separates Canaan from the wilderness, passing the northern lake, but never going west to the Great Sea."

As he spoke, his graceful hands traced the path of his travels through the air, as though upon an invisible map.

His voice was, again, wistful, as he spoke of his father.

"It was when we reached the border of the Galilee that Sidon left us," he said. "He never came on with us to this place, but felt it his destiny to return to the sea. The port of Sidon is named for him."

Ali nodded. "I knew it must be," he replied. "He was a mighty man, your father."

Melchizedek's lips curled in a smile. "I have always been grateful for the months we had together on that long journey. I knew, through that time, that he must have always loved me."

It came as a surprise to Ali to think of Melchizedek's needing a father's endorsement. It was hard for him to think of the old man as having ever been young.

But he had learned much he never knew. And he could have spent days more listening to the king's stories.

"When you came here, was it all you had hoped?" he asked.

"All, and more!" Melchizedek replied. "We knew the rock that crowns the valley must be sacred the moment we saw it. And the flowering hills, the Mount of Olives, ripe with fruit! We were in awe of the yellow stones and the garden that grew between them!"

The king clapped his hands together, pleased, these many years later, to recall his first impressions. "Oh, but it was the spring, bubbling and calling out to us from beside Kidron Vale, that convinced us all! Life could be sustained here. And we called the fountain "Gihon" for the river that flowed through Paradise!"

Ali was enraptured by the description. He had grown up here, but he had never so appreciated the beauty of Salem.

"You named the city 'Peace,' Master. You never had to conquer anyone to get it."

"That is true. And for a long time, now, we have maintained peace in our walls," he said, not without pride.

He caught himself. "We digress, Ali. We must save the story of Salem for another time."

With this, he glanced toward the east, where the tiniest hint of dawn was beginning, and stepped back into the chamber.

"This will be a demanding day," he said. "I need rest. So let us complete the story of Nimrod and the others. Where was I?"

"He was going to build a tower, Master."

"Yes," the elder said, rubbing his chin. "While my people were still building houses and planting fields, those of the eastern exodus were already laying the foundations of a temple to reach heaven."

Sadly he sighed, "Oh, Nimrod, if only your heart had been the Lord's, you would have had no need for a tower!"

—37—

Fifteen years after he entered Shinar, Nimrod sat atop the highest roof of his elaborate palace, his face shielded from the Tigris sun by a large, striped umbrella. Out across the plain, but still within the mammoth walls that slave labor had erected around the growing city, could be seen the beginning of a great foundation, the bituminous slab of the Tower of Shinar.

Though the population would not fill the city's established boundaries for many years to come, Nimrod's vision was for the future. Already smaller temples to numerous gods and goddesses graced the courts of Shinar's perfectly square streets and lanes. Sturdy bridges linked thoroughfare with thoroughfare over man made canals, crystal pools, and sanitary underground sewers. Flowered arboretums divided the city into park districts, and tunnels free from litter and congestion diverted traffic from the central markets. Palaces of the wealthy, three and four stories high, lent a majestic air to the broad avenue leading to the tower's religious compound.

The central boulevard, called the The Processional, lived up to its name, being frequently the site of royal parades and ceremonies.

Architects competed with one another to produce the most elaborate and artful designs. Artists vied to create the most tasteful ornamentation: winged bulls and dragons, lion-heads and sphinxes peered down from every balustrade, every arch. On each structure, color called to color for attention. Sunburned brick, the "stone" of Shinar, was burnished and gilded. It was enameled in scarlet, topaz, emerald, and sapphire, rivaling the gems of the richest mines and quarries, and contributing a luster to the city that would dazzle the most critical eye.

The day he first sat with his architects to draw up plans for the majestic tower, Nimrod had designated a site along the extreme north of the city.

Just this morning construction of the mammoth edifice was begun in earnest. It was a grand occasion, one awaited since the

142

Hamites had claimed the region a decade earlier. It was heralded with much pomp—a royal parade through the city square, an address from each of the three founding fathers, and then an elaborate breakfast prepared for all the foremen and their salaried crews. Slaves did not partake of the fine fare, but were served simpler food, doled out in generous portions.

Then off to work they all marched, shovels, picks, and trowels over their shoulders, whips snapping and a loud chorus escorting them toward the site.

A magnificent party was planned for evening. Every man, woman, and child, bond and free, would dance into the wee hours. At midnight, the congregation would gather around the tower's foundation. Beneath the full moon, the first spiral would be hallowed unto the gods. The blood of a virgin would be shed on the platform, symbolizing the people's commitment to give their best to the project and to the deities.

This moment Nimrod reveled in the sounds of industry echoing from busy shovels and pounding picks. All morning the cries of the masters and shouts of the workers had filled the air, bringing joy to the king's impatient heart.

Leaning out from beneath the fringed umbrella held over his head by a Shemite slave, Nimrod let the sun's full glory stream over his dusky face.

His mind was filled with visions of the gods descending and ascending upon the curving stairway that would months from now lead to the tower's top. He even scanned the sky in the faithful hope that, at some unexpected hour, he might catch a glimpse of their majesties.

Perhaps he could take it as a good omen that a shining black bird rode the currents above the distant work site.

Placing his hand to his breast, Nimrod clasped the obsidian raven nested there and watched the aloof swoops and turns of the glistening creature above.

Surely the gods approved his endeavors to reach them. Surely they would elevate him to a place of power higher than the peak of Shinar's tower.

—38—

B ecause there were no adversaries to the King of Shinar living in the Hiddekel corridor, the project of the tower and the ongoing building of the city at its base proceeded without impediment. No wars or uprisings threatened the progress of the region.

Within sixty months of the laying of the cornerstone, two entire spirals of the monstrous structure had been completed, covering many acres.

Since it was so wide at the base, it would never give the impression of its true height, even upon completion. It was projected to reach many hundreds of feet into the air, each of its ascending spirals recessed in turn upon the last. The top would boast a spacious and luxurious temple to the gods, and this, like the mystical heights of lost Olympus, would often be obscured by clouds.

In fact, the top of the tower would inspire as much mystery as the heights of great mountains in the north country. Already a royal priesthood was being prepared to keep and guard it, to dwell therein, never coming down except to pronounce the word of the deities that would surely be received atop its pinnacle.

Within its hallowed sanctuary, lunar and solar sacrifices would be made, curses and blessings would be invoked, and the petitions of Nimrod would be lifted to the sky.

Although the spirals would be smaller in circumference the higher up the tower they rose, each would take more time to complete than the last as the distance between each ascending level and the ground, where most of the materials were stored and formed, increased. Hours per day of manpower were spent in carting immense wheeled barges up the inclines to worksites along the curving layers. Engineers had stationed brick masons, cartwrights, and cement makers at intervals along the wide, snakelike ramp, where food, water, and supplies were in continual demand.

The entire project was expected to take between thirty and forty years to complete, even without interference. However, since this was a mere breath in the lifetime of most people, it was well worth the expense. Most of those who had seen its beginning would live to see its top lost in the clouds of the Tigris basin. Even if some were to die in the interim, they were told, anyone who gave of his wealth and his energy to the project would reap eternal benefits.

Of course, though there were no nations to bring armies against the plan, there were those within the system who took no pleasure in its goals. There were Shemite, Japhethite, and Canaanite slaves who detested the venture, not only because it robbed them of their youth and strength, but because they hated the heathen purpose to which each brick and each trowelful of mortar was dedicated.

Though they labored for the dreams of Nimrod, though they bowed the knee to Ham when he passed by in his gaudy chariot, or to the perfumed courtiers of Cush when they dallied and lisped together in the towering shadows, their toil exacted blood and tears, their families were trampled under foot, and no blessing from above was promised for their endeavors.

Perhaps even Yahweh had abandoned them. Perhaps He could not countenance their betrayal, though it was yielded at spearpoint.

Often, at night, upon the racks where they were quartered, when the dark enclosed each man to himself, their private prayers were raised for deliverance. Often Father Shem or Father Japheth would be remembered, and the God of Canaan would be petitioned.

But it seemed the sky was more attuned to the incantations of Nimrod's priests than to the pleas of Yahweh's people.

It was difficult to retain faith in a God who never answered. It was difficult to resist the allure of the tower, though it was formed by the hands of the slaves themselves.

With each passing year, the prayers of faithful captives grew fainter. And the shadow of the man made mountain grew longer across the land.

—39—

A s the years passed, when the people of Ararat remembered their lost brethren, it was with dwindling emotion. They had their own little empires to build, their own ambitions to pursue.

There were a scattered few, those who remained close to Noah, who retained a sense of prophecy, who managed to see beyond the shelter of their own small nations to a larger understanding of God's purposes. But such spiritual persons were rare.

Even Shem, while privy to the greater vision of his father, often struggled to maintain it amid grapplings for power and the lust of life that raged upon the mountain.

Had it not been for evenings at Noah's side, when he was reminded of things that had transpired upon the planet, of the unfolding drama that took in past and future, he would have slipped into the same mundane strivings as pulled at the ankles of men and women everywhere.

Since he was often confronted with his privileged status, with the responsibility that was his to keep the oracles of Yahweh, he knew there were greater things than gold or human success. Often, as the realms of exploration took in vistas farther and farther removed from the Ark's vale, he thought on Melchizedek and wondered what he might be doing.

Though he had never fully accepted the youngster's royal position when he governed Ararat, he had sensed his holy calling the day he departed. He sometimes pondered the purpose in God's summoning him away.

When he spoke to Noah of this mystery, the patriarch, seeing as a prophet sees, could discern the future only in snatches. Often his analysis took the form of repetition.

"Blessed be the Lord, the God of Shem," he would say, "and let Canaan be his servant. May God enlarge Japheth, and may Canaan serve them both."

• • •

One of the ways Noah helped Shem keep his spiritual focus was by passing on to him the duty of recordkeeping.

During the years of his ministry as prophet to Adlandia, and ever since the rains had come and gone, leaving a new world in which humankind could start again, Noah had kept copious journals. In fact, he had been a journal keeper since childhood, intuitively questioning whether it was wise to trust everything to oral tradition.

When he had designed the Ark, with the flexibility God had permitted, he had built storage compartments into the deepest holds, and there, unbeknownst even to his wife and sons, he had stored the dozens of journals and scrolls he had preserved since boyhood, now the only written evidence from the lost world.

As his life entered its final chapters, wisdom decreed it was time to pass on the legacy.

Shem would always remember when he received an invitation to spend several days with his father at Ahora. Since there was no birthday or feast to celebrate just then, Shem wondered what the purpose of such an extended stay might be.

It was late autumn. Harvest was over and the fields would lie fallow until spring. There was nothing pressing to keep Shem at home, and so, bidding Sindra good-bye, he set out from Sedeqetelebab.

When Shem arrived at Ahora, Noah was in a singular mood, somber yet eager, as though he had something very important to disclose to his firstborn.

Naamah, in celebration of Shem's visit, saw to it that the evening meal was as luxurious as any she could serve, and the villagers, all extended family of varying degrees, danced and made merry until midnight.

Only at bedtime did Noah hint at the purpose of the summons. Even then, he merely said, "Tomorrow morning we will go to the Ark. There is something there I want to show you."

At the crack of dawn, the old man roused Shem, handing him a walking stick and saying it was time for a hike.

Up the well-worn trail the two went, enjoying the crisp air and the low-angled rays of the sun. A wispy fog still cloaked the saddle-like gorge where the Ark rested. Material kept near the door for the making of torches was quickly bound together, and soon the men had a long, fire-lit stick to guide their way in the interior.

Shem followed Noah's cautious steps as he walked through the familiar corridors. Though the main door was kept shut when no one was around, there was no guarantee that wild animals had not crept in through cracks in the siding. They might not be so friendly as the ones who had originally been quartered here.

As the men walked further into the ship's hold, however, only small, skittering noises betrayed the presence of wee beasts, mice or rats disturbed by the invasion of light. When nothing more threatening revealed itself, Noah and Shem breathed easier, finding only curtains of cobwebs to be an impediment.

To Shem's bewilderment, Noah led him down two sets of stairs into the lowest level.

There was no true prow or stern, the ship being box-shaped, but since the family quarters were to the left of the door, they had always thought of the opposite end as the back.

It was to this end that Noah took Shem, and after several twists and turns they at last arrived at a small closet.

Shem could not remember ever having seen this nook of the Ark. The vessel was enormous, and he had little reason to recall each niche, though he and his brothers had helped to build it. Certainly they had had little occasion to venture into such a remote corner, when the ship rocked and heaved upon the Flood.

Brushing a mantle of webs away from the closet door, Noah lifted the latch and pulled the handle back. Creaking on rusty hinges, the well-made door slid open.

With mutual pride, the men marveled at their own handiwork. After years of settling, the jamb was still straight, and lintel square and true to the floor.

The ship did have a musty smell, as any old building would in a world damp as this new one. But to Shem's amazement, the closet's interior was dry and odorless.

Cautiously, Noah poked the torch into the hold. What met Shem's eyes was even more mystifying. Cradled among stacks of stuffed muslin bags were small boxes and pottery jars.

"Welcome to my library!" Noah announced.

Shem leaned inside. "Library?" he muttered, probing one of the bags with stiff fingers. "Where?"

"Careful!" Noah warned. "Those bags are full of salt!"

"Salt?" Shem asked. "Why?"

"To keep my scrolls dry. To preserve them!"

Looking more closely, Shem shook his head. "I still see no library, Father."

With a sigh, the elder reached in and drew out a jar from among the dozens that had ridden out the flood in cradled safety.

"Here," he said, removing the lid. "Do you see?"

"A scroll!" Shem enthused. "You mean all these jars contain scrolls?"

"Yes," Noah replied. "And the boxes have papers and journals . . . my diaries from the time I could first spell my name!"

Shem knelt inside the door, pondering the wealth of information deposited in this salty nook.

"The story of your life!" Shem gasped. "What a treasure is here!"

"Not just *my* life, Shem. The oracles and traditions of our forefathers, the story of the world from its beginning."

Shem was speechless. "How . . . when . . ." he stammered.

"I was always a notetaker, you recall," Noah laughed. "When I was a boy, after sitting with your Grandfather Lamech and the other elders around our evening fires, I would creep off to bed to write down the tales they told before I went to sleep. My mother was forever finding writings hidden in my drawers, on my shelves, under my blankets, anywhere I could stick them. She said I was smart to do this, but your grandfather would never have approved. He believed the oral tradition was sacred in its own right."

"Oh, Father," Shem sighed, "there is more here than could ever be preserved orally! Not with a hundred heads could a man rehearse all this!"

"Good, good!" Noah cried, slapping Shem on the back. "You appreciate my collection!"

"Appreciate?" Shem choked. "I am overwhelmed! So many times I have wished there was a record, a clear record of what the world was like! The young ones already doubt our stories of the overlords and the old times. Now, they can know, by your own account!"

At this, some of the sparkle left the prophet's eyes.

"I would like to think so," he said. "But men's hearts grow

colder by the day. Someday, all we know to be fact will be relegated to fable."

Shem hesitated to agree, but he knew the truth when plainly spoken.

"Besides," Noah went on, "I have spent years fending off souvenir seekers. If I had not done so, I fear this old ship would be nothing but a skeleton by now! If people knew these records were here..."

Shem nodded. They would have become the relics of looters and treasure seekers.

"So," the son asked, "what should we do with them, Father? Someday, neither you nor I will be here to protect them."

"That is why I have called for you," Noah replied. "I have given much thought to that problem."

He then set forth a plan, which, while arduous and time consuming, seemed the best way to preserve the chronicles. Shem would come to Ahora as often as possible to help Noah sort and classify the manuscripts. They would glean from them the most important stories to be transferred from the perishable scrolls to clay tablets. The archetypal tales, the one's most exemplary and symbolic of God's hand in history, would be committed to stone.

If they could find trustworthy scribes, they would enlist their help. But the most sensitive material would be of their keeping alone.

"We must then find caves, dry and remote, in which to hide them," Noah said. "When God wishes them to be brought to light, they will be."

Shem cleared a pile of salt bags and sat down, rubbing his knees.

"It is a mighty task," he sighed.

"Are you up to it?" Noah asked, with a wink.

"I am *honored*!" Shem exclaimed.

Surveying the urns and the boxes, he randomly pulled one out. Opening it, he drew forth a long scroll on which were many drawings, as well as words.

Wheel-shaped devices, some shooting fire, graced the parchment, along with street maps and elaborate buildings of many stories, arched gables and elaborate porticoes.

"The flying chariots and the cities of the gods!" he gasped. "Oh, Father, you have captured it all!"

"Here," Noah said, offering him another. "Remember these?"

Spread across this scroll were detailed representations of strange creatures—half-man, half-beast—or beasts composed of different species, the "hemi-boides" which were the products of Adlandian technology, and which had been destroyed by the Flood.

"My Lord!" Shem said with a shudder. "How could I ever forget?"

In a rush, all the wickedness and perversion of the old world cascaded through his mind.

"Surely mankind will never be so evil again!" he groaned.

Noah sat down beside him, poring over the parchment with memories of his own.

"The powers of darkness are never far away," he said.

Shem hunched down, thinking of the evil that already flourished in the new world. All too soon, the patriarchy of the planet would be left to him, the eldest son. He wondered if he would be so steadfast in the faith as his father had been.

Noah could see that Shem was overwhelmed. For a moment, he said nothing, wondering how he could help ease his son's fears.

Suddenly, a light came to his eyes. Reaching into a fold of his robe, he drew out a little leather pouch. "Of everything I have written, this is the most precious," he said.

He handed the pouch to Shem, who, opening it, found a small book. This, unlike the scrolls, was composed of pages, brittle, but still in good condition.

"What is it, Father?" Shem asked, almost afraid to handle it.

Very carefully, he leafed through the pages, finding yet other drawings, and many numbers.

"It is the instructions for the building of the Ark," Noah replied. "It is also the words of the Lord to me, as I ministered in those last days."

Incredulous, Shem gazed at the priceless pages. Intricate blueprints they were, with measurements and statistics for every detail of the Ark and the keeping of the animals.

"You often referred to this when we were building," Shem recalled. "I never thought much of it at the time."

Noah nodded. "I did not share it freely," he said. "My soul was still too tender, too new to the ways of God. I . . . I was often afraid of the work God had lain on my shoulders."

Shem sensed his father's sympathy. Noah was telling him he

understood the awesomeness of the calling he would be left to fulfill, and just how small he felt.

Gently, the old prophet pressed the notebook into Shem's hands.

"Keep it," Noah said. "Let it encourage you in the years ahead. But—" here Noah's voice cracked "—when I am gone, bury it with me. If in the future, men find my grave, they will find the book as well. They will know who I am, and they will know that the legends are true."

—40—

There came a day when the mysteries and the interpretations would be left to Shem alone, and to those who succeeded him.

A torrential morning rain had ceased, and the sun shone through a crystal clean sky as Shem made his way up from Sedeqetelebab to Ahora in answer to his father's summons.

The patriarch invited him to visit on a regular basis, but Shem was surprised that he should be called again so soon, since he had seen Noah only a few days earlier. He had no idea that when he arrived at the humble abode, he would find the usually lively man bedridden.

Nor did he know that Japheth and Canaan would be traveling up from the west in answer to the same call.

Shem sat beside his father's prone form, listening to his heavy breathing and holding his limp hand when the others arrived. So sudden it was, the swift descent of death's dark shadow. Noah, who had been vibrant with the pride of nine hundred and fifty years upon Earth, had within a matter of days succumbed to the tremors and frailty of old age.

Naamah held his head upon her lap, not lifting her eyes from his pale face when the men entered, but motioning them to draw near.

"He knows you are here," she whispered. "He would not go until you came."

Japheth knelt quietly beside the patriarch, and in that hallowed moment bid Canaan kneel beside him—father-in-law and son-in-law, for the first time, truly together.

Canaan could not contain his tears, but let them splash freely upon Noah's blanket. As he did so, the prophet roused from semiconsciousness.

Upon the face of Shem his gaze lingered, then it traveled to Japheth's somber countenance, and at last fell upon Canaan's bowed head.

153

"My sons . . ." he said faintly, laboring over each word, "the world is yours and the nations thereof. Between men of all places, there is no difference. Only remember . . . the first shall be last and the last shall be first."

The brethren did not take their eyes off him as he spoke. Though they did not fully understand his words, they listened respectfully.

"Every valley shall be exalted," he continued, studying Canaan's grief, "and every hill shall be brought low. He who would be master of all shall be your servant, and he who loses his life shall find it."

His breath came in rasps, now, and he perceived his wife's ageless face as through a mist. Her throat constricted, she bent over him, and kissed him lightly on the forehead.

Suddenly, he lifted his hands and sought the grip of his three off-spring. No further words would he utter. His lips, which had preached hundreds of sermons to a dying world, and which had communed with Yahweh along the shining sea-hills of the lost continent, would dispense not another syllable. But his face spoke volumes when he perceived that the ones he loved most were all within his grasp.

With one hand he stroked Naamah's soft hair, and with the other, he entwined three sets of fingers—Shem's of olive hue, Japheth's freckled white, and Canaan's, dark as gopher wood.

Peering out the window of his little cottage, he could see that through the sun-dappled clouds of last night's rain, a great bow arced above his mountain. The old ship, to whose purpose he had devoted his life, still sat silent and inviting upon the distant rise, and the valley of his people was this hour at peace.

Drawing his wife's head to his dry cheek, he breathed his last, and left the world to the children.

—41—

Hundreds of miles from the Ark, in the land to which God had led Melchizedek, in the land that lay west of Euphrates, west of the great desert, down the sweep of a smaller river, the King of Righteousness lurched out of sound sleep.

Sitting up on the tall bed that graced his chamber, he had just relived, in a dream, the day of his exit from Ararat.

Morning filtered on grey wings through the narrow arch of his room, and in the pale light he could see that his hands trembled.

He had had this dream before, and always it ended thus, with him awakening just as the silver tray, the bread and the wine, were being passed among the elders. Each time, as he handed the chalice to Noah, the vision vanished, leaving him in a cold sweat.

But something in the dream, this time, was different.

Swinging his legs over the side of the high bedstead, Melchizedek stood and paced the rich mosaic of his floor. He peered out from his portico, down toward Gihon, the tumbling fount that had first drawn him here.

The town, ranging the high walls of the little vale with pristine cottages and white stone fences, lay sleepy and quiet beneath the budding sunrise, crowned with an amazing flat rock called Moriah.

"Canaan" he had named this seaside land, for his grandfather. And "Salem" he had named the town—whose foundations had been of peace, as the name implied. Never had blood been shed here, except when he, priest of Yahweh, offered up an unblemished lamb for the sins of his people upon the tablelike crown.

No one here could know of the loneliness which had been his, year in and year out, as he had longed to sit again at Canaan's feet, or to plumb the depths of Noah's knowledge.

Thinking on the prophet, he rubbed his hands together, as if doing so might restore the details of the dream, which had vanished like thistle-down upon waking. Suddenly, the vision's alteration became obvious.

When he had reached out to hand the chalice to Noah, the patriarch had not been there to take it!

"Lord God!" he cried, running from his room into the hall. His guards, troubled by his strange behavior, bowed quickly as he passed and followed him down the corridor.

Anxiously, Melchizedek threw open the door to his courtyard and stumbled into the sunlight. Falling to his knees, he buried his head in his hands and wept aloud.

His ministers and attendants joined him on the pavement, hovering over him with concern and whispering among themselves. "Your Majesty," they inquired, "what ails you?"

At last, raising his tear-stained face to the sky, he leaned back upon his heels and cried in resignation, "The prophet is dead! Noah, the preacher of righteousness, has been gathered to his fathers!"

Nobody asked the source of his strange insight. They knew their king spoke with the unction of Yahweh. How they ached for his sorrow and longed to lighten his grief!

But he, looking up at them, shook his head. "Noah, the prophet, is dead," he repeated. "And the world is made poorer by his going."

—42—

The day the Tower of Shinar was to be completed, Nimrod emerged from his palace to the cheers of the city's thousands, the gleaming brass of his horned headdress catching sunlight and flashing golden rays across his face.

He stood on his courtyard's elevated porch, arms raised dramatically, and let the throng absorb his majesty as he posed before them.

His dark skin, oiled to a subtle sheen by the valets of his chamber, was exposed in torso and limb, his only covering a cascade of wide necklaces and intricate yokes adorning his breast, and a narrow loin cloth of gold embroidery slung between his spread legs.

In his hand he carried a bow-shaped scepter, symbolic of his titles, "Mighty Hunter of Men" and "King of the World."

His beard, which he had let grow for the occasion, reached to his chest and was crimped in ornate waves and braids, while his naturally curly hair graced his shoulders like a lion's mane.

Never, before or since the Flood, had a more glorious character walked through a more glorious city. As he stepped lightly down from his platform, the people fell with their faces to the ground, not moving until he and his long train of courtiers, priests, musicians, and ministers had passed.

Without a word he marched straight through town, trumpets blaring along the street called The Processional, cymbals crashing in cadence with his steps, until he reached the northern compound, where the colossal tower waited.

Armed soldiers, outfitted in resplendent scarlet costumes, their yellow, raven-crested banners unfurled above the crowd, held the masses in check as he strode by. So fervent was the throng's reception that at any moment the ecstatic worshippers could break rank, crushing in upon the king in crazed eagerness to touch him.

Nimrod had been warned that he should not go forth on foot. "At least ride upon your horse, if not in a chariot," his ministers pleaded. But the handsome monarch refused.

Forty years he had awaited this moment, and now that it had arrived, he would be close to the earth, to the hallowed clay of his city. He would walk the entire distance from the valley floor to the pinnacle of the newly completed tower.

There was not a soul of Shinar, citizen or slave, who was not present at this, the dedication of the edifice. Surely even the gods themselves would not stay away. In fact, it was commonly rumored that they would appear at the climax of the ceremony, when yet another virgin was offered atop the ziggurat's zenith.

Only the tower rivaled the king for majesty. More than a simple mound, it was a building of buildings, with doorways and arches leading off its wide spiraling ramp into a labyrinth of chambers and corridors, devoted to a multitude of purposes.

Storerooms and vaults held heaps of grain from years of harvest in the irrigated fields of Shinar's lush valley. Casks of oil and wine occupied yet other cellars and caves along the layered structure. Treasury rooms full of gold and precious stones were secured by bars and locks.

But there were countless holds deep within the mountain, which only the priests knew, and which were reserved for the secret rites and practices of their cult.

The roadway, curving along the multicolored cone like an entwining cobra, was so broad that three chariots could traverse it abreast, and yet there was still room along the curbs for wide flowerbeds, hanging gardens graced by small palms, budding trees, and even fountains.

Up, up the ramp Nimrod ascended, accompanied by hundreds of temple harlots, the holy men of all the Shinar gods, and his closest servants. So extensive was his train that at no point was it not visible as it circled the structure. And while the king traversed each layer, the cheers of the throng moved with him, a wave of sound going round and round the tower's base, as he came in view.

Between the color and pageantry of his entourage and the glistening spectrum of the ziggurat's multihued bricks, there had never been a sight to equal it.

It was planned that when the monarch reached the top and, with his priests, stood beneath the open sky, the final capstone would be placed atop the temple, thus ushering in the glory of the gods and a new age of conquest for Nimrod.

But first, before ascending the final terrace, while his voice could still reach the people's ears, he must turn and address them.

Stepping onto the deck on the last cylinder, he stopped his trek and raised his hands, calling for silence.

Music ceased, the dancing on the ramp stopped, and the huzzah of the people tapered to breathless suspense.

"My loyal subjects," he began, speaking through a megaphone, "you see before you this day the work of twenty thousand hands, and the result of ten thousand sacrifices. The great tower of our dreams, lifted to the gods!"

Mass emotion was piqued by his oratory. A resounding cheer rose again from the crowd, which had suffered under the duress of Nimrod's taxation for the sake of the tall temple.

Even the slaves, who had more reason to despise the structure than to adore it, applauded the end of the ordeal.

"For this purpose, we left Ararat's dark country. For this purpose, we traveled hundreds of miles and erected here our great city!"

Adulation rang through the square, and the cheer was, again, repeated.

"Because of our devotion, we are unified—one people, beneath one banner—never to be divided!"

At this, the guards along the route waved their standards, and the people roared agreement.

"Never shall we be separated, never lost among the unmarked miles of Earth! Forever, our nation shall stand, an emblem of prosperity and the blessings of the gods!"

Wave upon wave of shouts followed this, as the diverse crowd, spawned from seeds of war and captivity, swore allegiance to one another. The reality of their intolerant system, the memory of their inhumanity to one another, was suppressed amid the frenzy to accept Nimrod's word.

Somehow, with his charismatic phrases, he was able to lift them past their history to faith in the impossible.

"Look about you!" he cried. "See the great works of our hands! The roads, the walls, the palaces! This is only the beginning!" he asserted. "Today we have reached the stars! Our tower shall be called Babilu, 'Gate of Heaven!' For this it is! A door to the very throneroom of the gods!"

A nearly orgiastic outburst followed. But Nimrod was not finished.

"This we have begun to do," he declared, "and now there is nothing past our doing! Nothing which our minds imagine shall be impossible for us!"

Whether it was the rumble of drums among the musicians, or the stir of chariot wheels among the soldier ranks, no one could tell at first. But a tremor was shaking the ground as Nimrod punctuated his blasphemy with a flourish of his scepter.

The first time the ground trembled, nobody was concerned. But when the quaking was repeated, they began to whisper among themselves.

Nimrod surveyed the crowd with a stormy countenance. Standing with his ministers high up the monument, he did not feel the first rumblings. Anger etched his face at the nameless distraction.

But suddenly, he too felt something.

Turning to his governors, he noticed that they watched the ramp uneasily, as though it moved beneath their feet. Quickly, however, the king retrieved his composure and turned the omen into a happy sign.

"The gods!" he cried. "Feel their footsteps, my people! Surely they approach from the heights of heaven!"

Awestruck, the congregation peered toward the sun. Perhaps, indeed, the great ones were coming!

This expectation was rewarded by the clash of thunder and by the searing glare of lightning as it rippled out from a cloudless sky. In a thrill of wonder, the people fell back, watching as fingers of fire traveled down the ziggurat's side, sputtering along the ground in fiery tendrils.

But then, the miracle turned to menace as the temple's pinnacle was smitten again and again. Large chunks of enameled clay toppled from the altar house and crashed from level to level down the tower, shattering as they fell.

Now even Nimrod was afraid.

"Run for cover!" he cried.

But the people became only more confused.

"Flee!" he commanded.

They did so, but not in response to his order, for only a few among the crowd could understand his words.

In fact, as Shinar's panicked citizens stumbled over one another, trampling the weak and the small beneath heedless feet, they encountered only a confusion of nonsensical raving on every hand.

For some reason, which was beyond accounting, every fellow was to every other fellow a babbling fool, and every woman a lisping idiot.

Still the thunder roared, and lightning split the sky. It was noonday, and yet a pall of blackness cloaked the Earth.

Within moments the square had been vacated, and the streets were a clatter of lunacy.

As folks sought the sanctuaries of their own homes, they found a measure of respite, for the tongues were more kindred the closer people were in blood.

But even here, there was disappointment. Husbands and wives cried in broken syllables to one another, and children could barely understand their parents.

In the shadows of the viaducts, stranger avoided stranger. Paranoia ran rampant.

The walls of Shinar had become a prison, wherein a nightmare reigned.

— Interlude —

Dawn was creeping through Melchizedek's eastern window.

Ali sensed that the tale was drawing to an end. Yet, his head swam with a thousand questions.

"Master," he reasoned, leaning forward eagerly, "does this explain why there are so many languages in the world, and why people cannot understand each other?"

"It explains a good many things, my son," the king answered. "Most of all it explains that God will not be outdone. And it reminds us that all our plotting and all our pride only leads to frustration."

The lad gazed silently at the floor.

"So, what did the people do after that?" he asked. "Did Nimrod finally repent?"

Melchizedek smiled sadly. "Some folks never see the light. Some, when chastened, only stiffen their necks. But in the end . . . God always has his way . . . "

PART V

"So the Lord scattered them abroad from thence upon the face of all the earth . . ."

—Genesis 11:8a

The Dispersion

— 43 —

D
ust and rubble blew against the foot of the once mighty Tower of Shinar. Babilu, as Nimrod had called it, was now nothing more than an abandoned and crumbling husk, as was the shining city that had years before graced its shadow.

The streets lay silent beneath a parching wind, and the once lush, irrigated fields of the community spread desolate and abandoned far out from the dilapidated walls.

Travelers coming upon the wasted place reported from time to time that, listening carefully, they could still hear the industry and singing that had once filled the prosperous ruins. But, then, the Vale of Shinar had always been a site to spark the imagination.

It was a sad place now, its only life a memory.

For weeks after the bewildering confusion of the languages had mysteriously struck the populace, the citizens and the government had tried to bring order to the situation. But, never in the history of the planet, before or since the Flood, had the human race spoken with more than one tongue.

Oh, there had been faint linguistic differences in old Adlandia, and as always, when people had distance between them, they had various ways of saying the same things.

But there were no barriers to communication, such as existed suddenly and without warning between the Hamites, and between the tribal strains that made up their slave caste. Knowledge of how to transcend such barriers was an unknown art.

At last, in helpless frustration, the city being divided along lines of speech, the people began to leave town.

This exodus had none of the pomp and thrill of the previous one, when Ham and his nation had abandoned Ararat to pursue their glorious destiny. This time, the people took leave not only of a place, but of each other. Friends and coworkers, who had spent years together, following the same dreams and fighting for the same cause, were suddenly foreigners. Though they embraced upon parting, and though

167

tears flowed down their faces, they had no more communion.

And this time, they had no common destination. In fact, few of them could envision where they and their own families would settle.

There were those who returned to Ararat—especially the slaves who were no longer of any use to their masters, unable to take orders and give replies.

These, whose speech still favored the dialects of Noah and his valley, were received back upon the mountain, the answer to age-old prayers. Though decades had intervened, and though faith in their return had dwindled, the exiles had never been entirely forgotten.

Quickly they were absorbed into the growing communities of Ararat, their children adopting a nation that still worshipped Yahweh.

With wonder, the descendants of Shem, Japheth, and Canaan who had never left the mountain, listened to the tale of the great tower and the peculiar curse that had fallen upon it.

With the passage of time, whenever northerners referred to Nimrod's crumbled ziggurat, they made a play on words, calling it not Babilu as he had decreed, but Babel, or Babble. They did so with a twinkle in their eyes. For the mighty Gate of the Gods was no more, and Confusion was its nickname.

● ● ●

Although many of the Ararat remnant, once held captive in Shinar, returned to Noah's mountain, others took the fall of Nimrod's city as opportunity for adventure and as a chance to seek new territories.

Mingling with the tribes of Ham and Cush, who also sought new lands, they eventually took up their speech and were lost among the dispersed branches of mankind. Or if they did not mingle, they established their own nations and cultures in far-flung parts of the world.

As for the folk whose generations had never left the mountain, most of them, too, with time, branched north, south, east, and west— some retaining their heritage, and others blending in with the scattered of the Earth.

Eventually, so many languages and their variants, so many cultures and political entities existed, their boundaries fluctuating with the rise and fall of conquerors and treaties, that no one would be able to trace them perfectly.

In some dim way, however, they were divided along the lines of the original patriarchies, their linguistic styles falling roughly into three categories, depending on which son of Noah was their ancestor.

Though Nimrod and the Hamites of the Tigris Valley would never again attempt to pierce heaven with their buildings, they would not give up the desire for glory. The longing for Babilu, a gate to the gods, found its shadow in the founding of Babylon, and Nimrod also raised up the great city-states of Erech, Accad, and Calneh in the land of Shinar.

Then up from Babylon he went, to the Shemite land of Asshur, or Assyria, north of Shinar, and there he founded the incomparable Nineveh, and its suburbs—Rehoboth, Calah, and Resen.

For Cush was established the city of Kish, a variant on his name, and Nimrod's other mighty men each had a place and a nation: Ur, Eridu, Sippar, and so on.

Eventually, the name of Shinar corrupted to "Sumer," just as nation after nation rose in power and fell into unrecognizable decay.

Every one of these wealthy centers had its own tower to the gods. None was ever again so lofty or so presumptuous as the Tower of Babel, but the worship upon each was the same.

Yahweh was forgotten, for not even his hand of destruction, brought against the first city and its blasphemy, had produced repentance.

Such was the story across the Earth, as every little tribe pursued greatness and every man sought a piece of history.

—44—

As humanity and its many nations spread across the planet, there was, year after year, a small plot of land that was uncontested territory.

It was an international crossroads, and it was about whom there had grown up many mysteries.

His genealogy was not on any tribal roster. There were those who said he belonged to the line of Canaan, whom Noah had cursed.

Yet the aged one who dwelt in the little valley seemed to be beyond curses, beyond lineages and nations, as though he belonged to all those who knew of his existence.

Of course, all genealogies, by which the human race tried to define itself, were incomplete, containing gaps, some wide, some narrow, through which countless patriarchs had fallen from memory. For those who tried to identify the old man's line, this presented an impediment.

But the fact was that he had been in the region long before anyone else took up residence there, and no one knew his age.

Melchizedek was his name, "King of Righteousness," and he had founded the little city-state of Salem for his footstool.

Through the years, many other kings had conquered the territory surrounding the vale, but the old man did not seem to care. Furthermore, he had no posterity, never married or had a child.

Yet all those who traveled through his small town felt he was their father, if not in blood, somehow in spirit.

Perhaps herein lay the key to his mystery. For he, whose city had never gone to war nor shed the blood of fellow men, was more a priest than a king. As for himself, he said he had been sent to Salem, the "center of the Earth," to preserve the knowledge of Lord for all the world's inhabitants.

But while Melchizedek was a mystery to his fellow men, the world was no mystery to him. Like Enoch of old, he had outlived the comings and goings of empires. Though he still did not like to compare himself to that ancient sage, he had long ago accepted that Yahweh had a special purpose for his life.

Across the endless miles of the planet, once desolate of inhabitants, had sprung up innumerable families of man. Yet, as they came and went through his country, he knew their origins.

The tribes of the human race, isolated in distant corners of the Earth, were distinguished beyond mere linguistic and political variety. The appearance of people, itself, had taken on many changes. For the bloodlines, which altered according to dominant characteristics, also adapted for survival, accommodating climate and altitude, so that not only were skin colors different, but stature, and even the shapes of eyes and noses varied from place to place.

Yet Melchizedek, whose historical reference was older than others', knew that the folk of Earth were all children of the same fathers.

Though the descendants of Japheth would become known by many names, spreading northwest and northeast, to Europe and Asia, the old king saw in their fair-to-reddish skin and piercing blue or almond-shaped eyes the shadow of his great uncle.

From that son of Noah sprang those who would be called Europeans, Asians, Chinese, and Japanese, to name a few. The ruddier people who would eventually leave Asia and cross a northern strait would one day be Eskimos, and their kin would filter south to re-meet the whiter strain of Japhethites and be called Native Americans.

The Egyptians, the Babylonians and Sumerians, derived from Ham, as did the mighty seamen of Sidon's realm, who became the Phoenicians, and who went north, at least as far as the future realm of Ireland. Through Cush, Ham's children also sent a broad branch to the coasts and interior of yet another continent, to become the Africans.

From Shem was spawned the Persians, the Assyrians, the Hebrews, and the Arabs, to name a few, many of which were lumped together as "Semites." Melchizedek, when he thought of these, who either built mighty empires or roamed the Earth as vagabonds, remembered Noah's eldest son.

But Shem's destiny was yet to be fulfilled.

In fact, it was for the likeness of Shem that Melchizedek searched when his eyes lingered over the fields and roads sweeping past his little valley. From the day he left Ararat, he had known that their paths must one day cross again, and that in Noah's firstborn the fulfillment of God's final purposes resided.

EPILOGUE

<The Lord> "took away Melchizedek . . . from his father, and, after having anointed him as priest, brought him to <Jerusalem> the center of the earth . . . <where he> offered the bread and wine upon the altar . . . no one on earth knowing of his whereabouts until, at last, Abraham met him."

—Ethiopian Book of Adam and Eve 3:13 ff
(as explained by *The Jewish Encyclopedia)*
(Lore and Tradition)

". . . Melchizedek . . . King of righteousness . . . King of peace; Without father, without mother, without descent, having neither beginning of days, nor end of life; but made like unto the Son of God; abideth a priest continually. Now consider how great this man was . . ."

—Hebrews 7:1 ff

Melchizedek leaned back in his chair and closed his eyes, a mighty weariness overtaking him as he ended his chronicle.

Brilliant morning sunlight flooded the chamber, casting a golden blush across his ancient face.

Young Ali, who had sat up with the king through the whole night, was still wide awake, his heart charged with unflagging enthusiasm for the marvelous tale.

"Sir," he said, "all that you have told me, I believe! I know in my heart that you were there. And you have been in this land forever!"

"I have been here a long, long time," Melchizedek replied. "It was to this country that I was called when I left Ararat."

"And you named it Canaan, for your grandfather."

"That, I did," the storyteller nodded. "Many have longed to wrest it from the Canaanites, and so my people, wicked though they have become, are mighty in war."

Ali detected the king's sadness at the thought of this waywardness. Indeed, the Land of Canaan was far from the faith of Yahweh.

"So, Master," Ali considered, "That faraway look you sometimes get—it is for things yet to come?"

"There are promises still to be fulfilled," the old prophet said. "What God began in Noah, he has yet to complete. One day his land will be the possession of a holy nation."

Melchizedek rose from his seat and called for his elder steward.

Ali knew what was about to transpire. This was the Day of Atonement, and when the steward arrived, he bore a large tray of broken bread and a goblet of wine.

Before the king would leave for Mt. Moriah, however, where he would offer up his sacrifice, he exited his room and stood once again upon the balustrade of his palace wall. There he cast his gaze west, to the land of his father, Sidon.

Even after leaving Ararat with him, he had never been privileged to see the man much. It troubled him that Sidon's many descendants, through yet other sons, remembered him in legend only.

Legends were they all—the patriarchs whom the King of Salem had known in flesh and blood. When he contemplated his solitary position, it always made him tremble.

A breeze coming far inland from the coast caught his long white beard and blew it eastward across his shoulder. In response, he turned his vision toward the highway leading from the heights of Mount Hermon, and he remembered the mountain of the Ark.

At that very moment, a host of soldiers appeared on the highway that circled toward town from the north. The king's chamberlain, joining him on the wall, pointed enthusiastically at them.

"It is the army of Abram!" he cried, "They are returning from Dan! Word is that he routed the eastern alliance which has been troubling all of Canaan."

Little Ali, who had followed his master to the rail, stood on tiptoe, hoping for a glimpse.

"Yes, I have heard of him," the king recalled. "From whence does he hail?"

"He is a Hebrew, sir, from Mesopotamia," the chamberlain replied. "Son of Terah, of Ur."

Many Hebrews, and people of numerous nations, traveled through the crossroads region. But when the chamberlain made another observation, the matter took on a new complexion.

"Strange fellow, he is," he laughed. "Claims some nameless god has called him out of his homeland, to raise up a holy nation!"

Melchizedek suddenly straightened his shoulders, studying the servant carefully.

"A Hebrew, you say?" he repeated.

"Yes, Your Highness . . ."

"Arisen from the cursed land of Shinar, to fight against the sons of Babel?"

The steward gave a bewildered shrug, and Ali stifled a grin. The terms were obviously meaningless to the man, who had heard the Tigris region called Sumer, but not Shinar, and the eastern alliance called Babylonians, but not sons of Babel.

"Abram would be son of Shem!" the old monarch insisted.

"A Semite . . . yes, sir . . . I suppose he would be, as all Hebrews are . . ."

Again the servant was puzzled, not understanding the significance of such antiquated references.

Ali giggled softly.

But Melchizedek, carried away with the matter, was suddenly infused with an energy he had not known since youthful days in his grandfather's fields. Gathering up his robes, he descended the stairs toward the road, calling for his cloak.

"Bring the silver tray, as well!" he commanded. "We will greet the Hebrew at the gate!"

"But, Your majesty," the chamberlain objected, "he is a foreigner. Why do you stoop so low?"

"No foreigner!" the elder called over his shoulder. "He is kin! And I am not a king only . . . but a 'servant of servants' to my brothers!"

• • •

When Melchizedek went forward to meet Abram, one day to be called Abraham, beyond the gate of Salem, one day to be called Jerusalem, he took with him his tall shepherd's staff—the one with which he had once governed Ararat.

He knew in his spirit that the time of fulfillment had come, that the purpose of his royal priesthood and the guardianship of his holy vale could be passed on to another.

Within the vale, where Abram led his victory march, other kings came forth to greet the returning army, to give their thanks for his saving help, and to take the booty which he had retrieved from the eastern invaders.

With gracious etiquette he received their adulation, but when the Hebrew saw Salem's king approaching, he stopped still.

Something in the old monarch's gaze spoke volumes. It seemed that in his venerable and aged countenance could be read the mysteries of antiquity, if one only knew how.

When Melchizedek drew within arm's length, his snowy hair resplendent against a simple garb of white, and his ancient skin nearly translucent in the sun, Abram slipped down from his mount and bowed to the ground.

And when the old king's peculiar offering was brought forth, a silver tray, adorned with bread and wine, the young warrior partook in marveling silence.

He could not, just now, interpret the meaning of it. He could not know that Melchizedek relived, in the gesture, one of the most meaningful moments of this long life.

Nor could he know that one day one of his own descendants would perform such service for the sons of Shem, and all their younger brethren.

"Your Majesty," Abram said at last, his voice quaking, "to you I give a tenth of all the spoils of war!"

The king surveyed the Hebrew's suntanned face, appreciating its sturdy features, so reminiscent of Noah's firstborn.

"Blessed be Abram of the Most High God," the wise one pronounced, "Possessor of Heaven and Earth. And blessed be the Most High God, who has delivered your enemies into your hand."

Abram, who had many questions, was speechless, and could do nothing but bow low again. As he did so, he perceived that Melchizedek sighed, as though a great burden had been lifted from him.

Then, stepping even closer, the ancient priest placed a frail hand on Abram's shoulder. With no explanation, he handed his shepherd's staff to the descendant of Shem and turned away.

Silently, not looking back, he trekked toward the hill of Salem, up toward Mt. Moriah and its fabled rock.

There the old monarch seemed to see the patriarchs waiting— their hands outstretched to receive him.

Noah was there, with Shem and Japheth.

And beside them stood Canaan, whom Melchizedek hailed with a smile.

"Now of the things which we have spoken this is the sum: We have such a high priest, who is set on the right hand of the throne of the Majesty in the heavens . . . a priest forever after the order of Melchizedek . . ."

—Hebrews 8:1; 7:21b

"O Jerusalem. . . . In it are the chosen of his servants. From it the earth was stretched forth and from it shall it be rolled up like a scroll."

—*The Hadith*
(Lore and Tradition)

About the Author

Ellen Gunderson Traylor is a gifted storyteller whose novels bring the most memorable characters of the Bible to life. Together, her books have reached more than half a million readers. Ellen lives with her family in Montana.

• • •

Read the exciting sequel to *Melchizedek*
Jerusalem—the City of God

Other Books by
Ellen Gunderson Traylor

Esther
Joseph
Joshua
Moses
Samson